VISION, VALUES AND VELOCITY
BY SAM PITRODA

Published by:

siliconindia

37600 Central Ct., Suite 212
Newark, CA 94560

www.siliconindia.com

Contact Sam Pitroda at: pitroda@corp.siliconindia.com
Contact siliconindia at: editor@corp.siliconindia.com

ISBN 0-9716367-0-2

Printed in the United States of America

Vision Values & Velocity

BY SAM PITRODA

CONTENTS

All illustrations by Sam Pitroda

FOREWORD

An hour a month. That's what Mr. Sam Pitroda promised to give us when we met him in his office in Sanchar Bhavan in New Delhi in January 1997. *siliconindia* at that time was merely a concept in our minds, and this commitment of time from Mr. Pitroda was a major coup towards making this concept a reality.

From then to now, November 2001, *siliconindia* has become the most widely circulated and respected international magazine and Web site targeting South Asians worldwide. It is a bridge between the U.S. and India, providing valuable content and services to over 250,000 readers around the world. *siliconindia* also organizes more than 25 conferences a year, attended by 10,000 professionals. Month after month, we have published more than 45 Sam Pitroda Columns, which have become a pillar of the growth of the magazine, its agenda and vision. Since the beginning, we have received thousands of messages from readers about the column – critical and appreciative, but most importantly expressing how the articles touched a deep chord in their hearts and minds. The articles have addressed a common but difficult pain-point, articulating readers' own feelings about their home country, sparking debates about important issues that often get neglected, or motivating them to go into uncharted territories. Dozens of readers have written to us about how the column has inspired them to take their life and career to a new level – be it going back to India to work for a non-profit organization, changing careers, starting a new company, revising the way they work with people above and below them in an organization, and so on. It is this widespread response and support that has kept us going, often against seemingly impossible hurdles created by the combination of severe print deadlines, and Mr. Pitroda's very tight schedule.

In putting together the column over the past several years, and now recreating that rich content in the form of this book, I want to thank all the individuals who have contributed at various stages, including the entire *siliconindia* staff – writers, copy editors, proof readers and graphic designers; and Mr. Pitroda's family and aides. It has been a privilege for all of us to work with Mr. Pitroda to produce the column and the book. The depth of his experience and perspective on all matters – business, economic, political, technological and social – is remarkable, and it has been truly rewarding for us to bring it out in the shape and form of the column and now this book.

And finally I want to thank Mr. Sam Pitroda himself. He had the vision and faith to recognize that we hoped to achieve something meaningful when we first went to him with the idea. Over the course of the years we worked with him, he has had the patience and belief in the power of our combined message. He took our calls in various parts of the world at odd times, took quick breaks in meetings to review article drafts we sent him, and helped us devise new content, not only for his column, but for the rest of the magazine itself. Beyond all of this, without his spirit, mindshare and trust in our conviction and capabilities, neither the column, nor this book would have been possible.

We hope this book helps you to put into perspective the joys, challenges, concerns and conflicts of dealing with India and being Indian; and provides guidance on simple but crucial and neglected management issues faced by all of us on a day-to-day basis. This encapsulates the mission this book hopes to serve. We look forward to continuing to bring out the column and more books in years to come. In the meantime, we would all appreciate your response at: pitroda@corp.siliconindia.com.

Yogesh Sharma
Editor, siliconindia

Yogesh Sharma & Sam Pitroda

PREFACE

On the eve of August 15, 1947 – the day that marked India's freedom from 300 years of British rule, Jawaharlal Nehru delivered his famous "Tryst with Destiny" speech:

"Long years ago we made a tryst with destiny, and now the time comes when we shall redeem our pledge, not wholly or in full measure, but very substantially. At the stroke of the midnight hour, when the world sleeps, India will awake to life and freedom. A moment comes, which comes but rarely in history, when we step out from the old to the new, when an age ends, and when the soul of a nation, long suppressed, finds utterance. It is fitting that at this solemn moment we take the pledge of dedication to the service of India and her people and to the still larger cause of humanity."

It was Nehru's independence speech that molded the theme for the 1997 Network of Indian Professionals (NetIP) conference in Washington, D.C. I was invited to deliver a keynote speech at this conference, which was filled with bright, beautiful and dynamic Indian youth. Their enthusiasm served to motivate me, and I talked about everything from meeting my wife for the first time, to working with Rajiv Gandhi on technology missions, entering the often bureaucratic and challenging systems of India and finally succeeding in building a network of Public Call Offices to provide every citizen with access to communication. By the end of my speech, I felt as if the energy in that room could change the world.

It was also at this conference that I reconnected with Yogesh Sharma, editor of *siliconindia* magazine, six months after meeting him for the first time in New Delhi. *siliconindia* had just come out with their inaugural issue that included my first article in the magazine, based on the interview I had given to him in my first meeting. There, he reminded me of my commitment to give him an hour a month, based on which they would generate a monthly column. What followed were many engaging and enlightening conversations and speeches, resulting in more than 45 columns, intense interaction with individuals from around the world interested in India and management, and finally, this book.

I have deeply enjoyed talking to the editors at *siliconindia* and the larger audience that I am able to reach through its readership. The editors who spent their time on these columns often had to chase me across various countries and many time zones for our phone conversations. In the end, it was well worth it and I have received a lot of very thoughtful comments and concerns from the readers. Unfortunately, it was not possible for me to respond individually to each letter.

Every topic we have covered in this book is one that is close to my heart, and I am thankful to the magazine and its subscribers for this opportunity. I hope that many of our young people pick up the topics and ideas that I have expressed, for they are the ones who can make a difference in the lives of millions. My overwhelming message to the readers has been that information technology in India and the rest of the world touches all basic human needs, and should be made more relevant to development globally. There are a variety of interpretations to my message, as there are a variety of ways in which young, bright individuals can give back to the country of their origin. And from the response I received at the NetIP conference and from my column, we have succeeded in creating this pool of educated and energetic youth that are concerned about and committed to bringing about positive change in India and globally. Personally, the 10 years that I spent in India were the best and most fulfilling years of my life. They have both changed me, and those around me. There is, however, much work remaining to be done.

I have received an overwhelming response to my column from the readers of *siliconindia*, and this book is in response to that enthusiasm. I hope that we can, as Nehru said in his speech on Independence eve, "Step out from the old to the new," forever maintaining our commitment to the service of humanity.

Sam Pitroda

ON **INDIA**

India is a very complex country – one that is very difficult to manage and assess. The modern and the ancient converge here like nowhere else. India possesses much history, material prosperity, cultural prosperity, social and political conflicts, struggles of development, achievements and excellence, and continuing poverty. In spite of providing this world with major religions, non-violence as a tool for social change, advanced mathematics and more, India continues to be a country of high illiteracy, increasing population, very high unemployment, poor infrastructure and a predominantly rural agricultural society. When I look west from India, I look at Africa and it feels like we have done something worthwhile in the last fifty years. Then I look east to Hong Kong, Singapore, Malaysia and Indonesia, and I know that we could have done a hell of a lot more.

To begin with, India must be praised for what we have achieved in the last fifty years. We have built a thriving democracy out of a poor, populous and socially divided region. In India, 400 million people vote and governments change peacefully. But the rest of the world has moved too fast and too far for India's record. Can we really achieve what the nation set out to do 50 years ago – to end poverty, ignorance, disease and inequality of opportunity? Our record of democracy may be worth bragging about, but our record of social inequality or economic prosperity is not something to be happy about.

How can Indians in India and abroad progress from words to actions? First, we must inform ourselves and learn more about India. We should connect with other Indians all around the world who want to contribute to India and try to understand what they are trying to do. Results may be slow to come by. Everything that you have learnt in your MBA program does not always work in India. However, you still need that foundation. These are the contradictions of India. What you need is not necessary; what is necessary, you do not always need. It sounds a little crazy. But that is India and her mind-set. To do anything meaningful in India, you need inner strength, conviction and courage. You need to internalize your concerns for the country. This process may take a long time. Why do you have to do it? Because you feel you have to do it.

In this first part of this book, I present my various perceptions of India - her people, motivations, institutions, character, machinations, qualities, future potential and what will bring her up on both national and international arenas.

GANDHI FOR THE NEW MILLENNIU

| *Gandhi was a great communicator and leader. What can he tell us today?*

Gandhi, the father of the Indian nation, worked for the independence of the country and mobilized the masses, ultimately leading India to freedom. That was 54 years ago, and now he is essentially forgotten in India. We have put Gandhi on a pedestal only to look up to him every once in a while. Contradictory as it may sound, if you ask an average student in India who their role model is, they would most probably say Gandhi. Yet, because Gandhi is so high up in concept, you really cannot relate to him. Until Richard Attenborough's movie was released, Gandhi was forgotten in the Western world as well. The movie made people aware of Gandhian values and principles, not just Gandhi the person, but Gandhi the phenomenon. The qualities that Gandhi epitomized need to be revisited today.

Communication

Gandhi was the greatest communicator that ever lived. Using very simple symbols and actions, he communicated very complex messages to create a mass movement. But in this age of high-tech communication, our leadership fails to convey their vision, whether it is at the political, social or even corporate level. Gandhi was a master of media.

Going forward, several messages need to be communicated. For example, "India is going to be a software giant," "India will be a global economic power" and "India will be completely liberalized." These messages can be simplified, packaged differently and conveyed to the masses, as Gandhi proved possible. The message must appeal not just to the media-aware elite, but also to the public at large, in their own language and style.

Untouchability

Gandhi constantly emphasized equality. He propounded breaking up of caste, gender and age barriers, as well as abolishing untouchability. He showed love and companionship toward people from every part of society. Everyone had a place in his scheme of things. Today in India, we must remind ourselves that nothing and no one is inferior. Even in the business world, the boundaries that have been created around businesses are no longer needed. Today, a competitor could be a potential partner; employees and suppliers can be shareholders. The more we focus on these concepts, the faster will be our rate of growth.

Take the mission-critical case of literacy and education, for instance. In India, religion could play a key role in this endeavor, but has not. Temples, mosques and gurudwaras should begin to provide literacy classes to the people, knowing that such a large percentage of the population is illiterate. Indian people have great faith in religion, which can be utilized toward this cause if religious leaders take this as a task. This is an extension of Gandhi's tirade against the concept of untouchability. Being an untouchable meant you had no access to opportunity and being illiterate is the same thing in a rapidly developing world.

Perseverance

Gandhi never gave up. He got beaten and bloodied; yet he stood back up on his feet and continued to fight for what he believed in. Once he made up his mind that India would put up a fight to obtain her freedom, he just kept at it. I think one of our problems right now is that we have not made up our minds as to whether or not we want to modernize India. The perseverance that is required to be able to galvanize the country died right after Independence. The same values that attained freedom from colonial rule are required to build a modern nation, but these values have not been channeled toward this new goal. China, for instance, developed a successful four-point program for modernization; the only difference is that they kept at it for 25 years. India, today, does not show that tenacity, whereas Gandhi did.

Simplicity

This was perhaps Gandhi's greatest characteristic, and it is extremely relevant to India's situation today. Simplicity is not about wearing white khadi clothes. Consider our politicians today – they have five commandos around them wherever they go. Simplicity is about people in public offices minimizing personal requirements until the people around them have reached a minimum standard of living. Extravagant living by people in public office does not go unnoticed. Simplicity amongst corporate leaders in India is equally important because the difference between the top and the bottom level is much larger and noticeable than in other countries. For example, in the U.S., employees who sweep the floor or take out the garbage may also own a car, a TV and other amenities that workers of a similar profile in India do not have access to. It is difficult to expect high quality work from someone who perhaps lives in a slum, barely survives with the salary he gets and travels one and a half hours to get to work, sweating in the heat. Companies need to bring the standard of living of their employees up to a point that they can begin to appreciate their quality of life before bringing quality consciousness to their work.

Related to simplicity is the concept of self-reliance. This trait is often misconstrued as closing the doors to the outside world. Self-reliance is about adding value at home —using only what is already available. When we were working in India to produce rural telephone switch, people said: Why do we need to develop this in India, when it can be bought for cheaper outside? Well, according to that line of thinking, we need not produce anything since pretty much all of it can be bought for cheaper outside. But technical talent was available in India, and we had to provide this talent with a mission to create something unique and useful. This was a concept that Gandhi promoted, although at that time the means that he used were different — he urged people to burn foreign goods. More than anything else, that was a communication exercise, yet it conveyed a message of self-reliance throughout the country.

Truth

Gandhi stood for truth and absolute truth. With information technology, this becomes a greater reality because IT brings in openness, accessibility, connectivity and information for anyone, anywhere. The convergence of truth and information is going to be the foundation for a modern India in the new millennium.

In the final analysis, Gandhi talked of rural development and a self-sufficient community, two things that we could not translate or fulfill after him. As a result, people from villages moved to urban areas for jobs, power, water, transport and other advantages. With the Internet and other information technologies, I think it is possible to make rural India self-sufficient. If you look at the history of the last 100 years, most of the new towns were built along the railroad. In the United States, businesses bloomed near the convenient eight-lane highways. The next round of prosperity will come from Internet highways. Creating new Internet infrastructures that run through rural India will enable people to do work and business from wherever they are, reducing the load on several, already stressed, systems. By using new technologies to provide everything at our fingertips, we may see people moving back to where they came from, and to the advantages of cleaner air, uncongested streets and a better way of life.

Incidentally, during a visit to the Gandhi Ashram in Sabarmati, Gujarat, I discovered a distressing situation. The ashram does not get enough funds from the government for even basic maintenance. Gandhi's story, his letters and a lot of other archival material are stored in rather poor condition at the ashram. It would be a good idea to modernize the ashram and make its resources available on the Web. This way the material would not only be preserved better but also more people will have access to them and benefit from them.

Gandhi is more relevant today than ever before. Gaining independence from the British was simple — the enemy was clearly identified and was essentially external. Modernization is much more difficult, because the enemy is unidentifiable and engrained within the system. Just as Gandhi created the drive for independence into a movement, modernization needs to be provided with this same breath and force – with a missionary zeal.

■

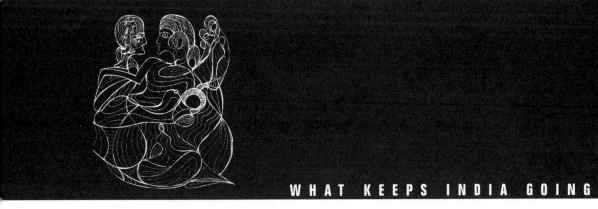

WHAT KEEPS INDIA GOING

Should the many problems India has - widespread illiteracy, frequent power breakdowns, sanitation and water problems, unreliable telecommunications infrastructure - deter foreign investors or corporations from doing business in India? Not at all. The trick is to get inside the skin of the country to understand what keeps it going.

Despite India's problems, the country offers many opportunities to potential business partners who can look beneath the surface. When they do so, they inevitably see a land whose people and institutions endure. India perseveres despite daunting challenges, without civil wars or riots.

What keeps it going?

People often compare China with India. China is very calm on the surface. Everything seems to be working. The society is highly organized. People lead orderly lives. But below the surface, China is seething. The people are discontented with the system. With ambition thwarted and personal drive dampened, radical ideas are constantly brewing.

India, on the other hand, presents the opposite impression. On the surface it is chaotic. Nothing seems to work. Everyone is frustrated with bureaucracy. There are long lines for essential items, shortages and inefficiencies. But at the same time, beneath the surface, all is calm. Life goes on, as if none of the chaos matters. Despite the problems, the tranquility at the lowest levels keeps India going. Where does this really come from and what does it really mean? There are several key reasons for this character of the Indian nation.

The first is **diversity**. India is a continent in and of itself, not just a country. As a result, even with a population of a billion people, India is self-sufficient in its basic needs. It unites different peoples, cultures, customs, foods and cuisines, musical tastes, styles and so on. Over time, people have become used to the differences and to the diverse environment. India has absorbed many external political, social and cultural influences, without discarding anything.

The second element is **simplicity**. Typically, India has not been a highly materialistic society. For most of the population there is no such thing as separate beds for children, or separate rooms for everybody. People often sleep on floors or wherever space is available. In a large part of rural India today, the concept of "my room, my possessions, my requirements" is foreign to families. As a result, life is very simple, at least in terms of material goods. But it is rich in terms of rituals and customs. For example, prayers in the morning, or the timing and style of routine matters such as bathing and eating.

The third factor is **personal laws**. People in India derive deep spiritual sustenance and support from close family ties. Indians form primary bonds very easily, and this results in strong personal networks. Networks of connections, with relatives and friends, are tied together by customs and procedures, based on personal laws that everyone follows. People don't like to go beyond these boundaries. In India, people may have difficulty following public laws, but the personal laws are honored at all times. On the other hand, these also create boundaries, constraints and pressure to follow certain habits.

Traditionally India's personal networks have been based on caste. But now they extend beyond caste, religion and professions. People have always respected age and seniority. As a result there is always a fear of what elders, neighbors and communities might think. That sets up barriers to how things are done, and indeed to determining what needs to be done.

Good and Bad

While this situation has many benefits, there are bad effects as well. Since life is very rigid, people don't take risks, and they don't innovate. Life remains very comfortable. Indian traditions are replete with the everyday wisdom of personal rituals, yoga, music, dance, food and religion. Many of these traditions have evolved to create inner peace and contentment. Consequently, Indians are not very ambitious. Unlike many other countries, India has never invaded its neighbors in a self- aggrandizing effort. The concept of karma is a reflection of this — you have certain duties to perform, and you perform them, without worrying about the result. Do what you can. If you don't finish, you can come back in your next life to complete it. Thus there has never really been any concept of time or deadlines — extrapolating in the *chalta hai* mentality — and of course it's okay if it is not perfect. All of these things together create a mindset of serenity and harmony that keeps India going despite all the changes on the macro level.

Consequences

A result of this is that neither national nor international politics have much of an effect on family and community life in India.

But what about businesses entering the Indian market? Primarily, the lack of a sense of urgency in the country prevents work from getting done as fast as it might in another country. Nevertheless, India is a huge and diverse market, with far less competition and far more opportunities for creating efficiencies and better products.

Sure, sometimes projects or tasks aren't completed on time. But executives looking to expand their operations internationally should keep an important fact in mind: India, despite its many problems, is a stable place to do business. There are no civil wars and democracy has sustained itself, and there are no large-scale disruptions, despite the diversity. Compare this to the upheaval we have witnessed all over the world in similarly diverse countries — the Koreas, Ireland, Eastern European countries such as Yugoslavia and Russia, and many more nations. From that perspective, India with its billion people has been extraordinarily calm!

The Effect of Technology

Technology's primary impact is to increase the aspirations of the people. They see the enhanced lifestyle on TV, for instance, and decide they want the same good life. In villages it is common to see women wearing lipstick while working in their farms, and men wearing shirts instead of kurta pajamas! This would have been a joke 20-30 years ago — but now it's acceptable. And look at the huge market for shampoos and soaps in India, sold primarily in pouches, something that you will never see in the Western world. The reason is simple — pouches are easier to distribute, and people don't have to spend a lot of money to buy a bottle.

Other effects of technology are apparent all over the country. Technology increases market potential and demand, introduces efficiencies, better distribution systems, and facilitates mobility and shrinks distances. These in turn are creating newer versions of the personal laws, rituals and habits mentioned above. This will lead ultimately to a strong global culture in India, which will co-exist with the local culture.

■

COMFORT AND STRENGTH IN CHAOS

Technology is changing our lives dramatically, but in the process it is also creating unforeseen chaos. In this new topsy-turvy world, Indians seem to be at ease.

The spur of activity in the technology arena — mega mergers between media and Internet companies, firms running with no profits in sight, companies giving away goods and services for free and still being valued at an ungodly multiplier created chaos in traditional business understanding.

Information technology has become pervasive, creating a lot of new challenges to traditional business processes. The way we do business has changed considerably and is still changing. We are finding new ways to do old things. Examples include activities such as shopping, electronic banking, business, education, telemedicine and library research. We all know that distance is dead. What used to be far is near, what is local is global. As a result of all this, we are going through chaos of the first order.

Comfort in Chaos

How do people and society cope with such chaos? A lot of them are struggling. Indians, I think, especially those in Silicon Valley and the high-tech industry, are doing well the world over because they are generally comfortable with chaos.

Be it Mumbai or a village in Punjab, people are wearing all sorts of different dresses. Some women are in saris; some in salwaar and kurtas, men wear different types of suits, or plain dhotis, some in colorful turbans or headdresses. Different cultures, music, dances and paintings abound. Although we constantly talk of "unity in diversity," I would like to call it a celebration of diversity. If you look hard, you will see that diversity itself creates a certain amount of chaos. It also teaches one how to live in chaos.

The Eastern Edge

Technology has brought about social transformation and diversity in a country like the United States. Everything is changing. In the 1960s, when I came to the U.S., white-collar workers were just that – white. Now, Asians hold 30 percent of these jobs. It becomes obvious if you walk into any bank in the United States. It is a colorful mosaic of diversity. People come from different countries and cultures, and consequently they differ in the way they dress, the way they work, the way they analyze things, the way they present problems and in just about everything else.

Even the early idea that American companies solve American problems is no longer valid. Earlier, American companies were seen as simply exporting Coke, Nike shoes or other American products. But now these companies and their executives are being affected by the foreign cultures to which they are exposed. For example, Coca-Cola has been influenced in some ways by Indian styles of advertising and Indian tastes. What we are seeing today is true globalization. When this kind of globalization happens, there is a certain amount of chaos.

If you are not comfortable in this kind for environment, it is difficult to function and difficult to adapt. The Western mind thinks in compartments and is very structured and well organized. This clearly explains in part the success of western civilizations. Everything is black and white. But it is not used to chaos and cannot function seamlessly in such conditions. But technology has challenged traditional structures and the key now is to gain a level of comfort in a system that is not organized, and always changing.

In the new scenario, it is a lot easier for Indians because we have grown up differently. I think part of the success of Indians technocrats and entrepreneurs the world over comes from the fact that they have grown up in chaos, learned to live in chaos and actually can draw comfort from chaos. Living in chaos gives you the ability to deal with multiple variables. I think it is a great value that we have not recognized in ourselves. On account of our upbringing, we can recognize the strengths in people, their values and also accept people and cultures the way they are, instead of trying to change them.

These qualities translate into tangible advantages in the workplace, and to my mind is a major strength for Indian professionals in Silicon Valley. When everything known is challenged and being changed, Indians do not feel challenged, they feel comfortable.

Indians are able to adapt and work better in multinational teams because they accept diversity as a part of life and are used to it. We need to recognize this strength and celebrate it. We are reaping the benefits of this quality in us. I wish we could take some of this back home and bring attention to the fact that an Indian upbringing has become a source of strength in high-tech places such as Silicon Valley.

I believe that Indians will rule the 21st century in technology not only because of their engineering and entrepreneurial skills but also because of their ability to function in chaos.

THE MAGIC OF TEAMWORK

One Indian = 10 Japanese in talent, 10 Indians as a team = One Japanese. Lack of teamwork and cooperation is one of the most serious problems affecting progress in all areas of India, and wherever Indians work worldwide.

The key problem in India has always been implementation, not a lack of policies. We have great policies and ideas about how to do things, but somehow these things do not get done. The main prerequisite to successful implementation is teamwork, and yet I find this severely lacking in the Indian way of working.

When the Japanese came to work in India to develop the Maruti Suzuki car, a joke went around that one Indian was equal to 10 Japanese: Indians were very smart, capable and dedicated individuals. But 10 Indians were equal to one Japanese: Indians lacked team spirit and cooperation. And that truly sums up the situation regarding our team skills.

What makes matters even worse is our "crab" mentality - if someone is trying to climb higher and achieve more, others just drag him down. The signal that a lot of Indians send out is, "I won't do it; I won't let you do it; and if by chance you start succeeding, we will all gang up and make sure that you do not get to do it."

The question is: Where does this attitude come from, and how do we recognize and handle it?

Hierarchical System

Part of the problem is our cultural background. Our traditional system claims that whoever is senior supposedly knows best. This was fine in earlier times when knowledge and wisdom were passed on orally; but in modern society, there is no way that one person can know everything. Today, you may find that a young computer-trained person has more answers for an accounting problem than a senior accountant. Until we understand how best to leverage this diversity of experience, we will not be able to create and fully utilize the right kind of teams.

In my younger days in America, I attended an executive seminar for Rockwell International, where about 25 senior company executives had congregated for a week of strategic discussion. In the evenings, we would break out into five different groups of five people each. In these group workshops, someone would delegate tasks, saying: "You make coffee; you take notes; you are the chairman; and you clean the board." The next day, there would be different duties for each group member. No one ever said, "But I made coffee twice." I thought to myself, if this were happening in India, people would be saying, "But I am the senior secretary - why should I make the coffee and you be the chairman?" Hierarchy comes naturally in our minds.

What Derails a Team?

Group work requires a thorough understanding of the strengths and weaknesses of individuals irrespective of their hierarchy. Because of our background, we often do not learn how to exercise and accept leadership – to lead and follow – simultaneously. Some gravitate toward exercising leadership, and others gravitate toward accepting the lead of others. But in true teamwork, everyone needs to do both. Being a good team player implies respect for others, tolerance of different points of view and a willingness to give. The ability to resolve conflicts without either egotism or sycophancy is a very important aspect of being a team player: you have to agree to disagree.

I find that people in India somehow tend to focus on achieving total agreement, which is almost always impossible. So before work begins, people want everyone to agree on everything. Instead, they should say, "This is what we agree on, so let's start working on this. What we do not agree on, we will resolve as we go along." For things to move forward, it is important to work on the agreed-upon aspects and not get bogged down in areas of disagreement.

Yet another snake that kills teamwork is people's political agendas. You have got to be open, clear and honest to be a good team player. Most people though, have a hidden agenda – they say something but mean the exact opposite. I call it "split-level consciousness." To say and mean the same thing is a very critical part of a good work ethic.

Criticizing the Individual or the Idea?

In my days at C-DoT (Centre for Development of Telematics), when there were 400 employees, I asked an American psychiatrist to come to India as a consultant and give me a report on the "psychological health of C-DoT" – something that had never been done before in India. He spent several days in the organization and talked to a lot of people, trying to understand the situation. His analysis opened my eyes to a lot of things I did not realize because all my life I had worked in America. People complained to him that I was ruthless and criticized them in front of everyone else. And until then I had thought that I was simply being open. If someone had not been doing well, I would tell him or her to his or her face in a general meeting. The employees said that was insulting, and that they should be pulled aside individually to be told of their inefficiency. But in today's world, you cannot afford to do that every time. Besides, I figured that offering constructive comments to someone in a meeting was for the benefit of all present, and everyone could learn from that individual's mistakes.

It was then that I learned how Indians do not differentiate between criticizing an idea and criticizing an individual. So in a group, if you tell someone that his idea is no good, he automatically takes it personally and assumes that you are criticizing him. No one can have a good idea every day on every issue. If you disagree with my idea, that does not mean that you have found fault with me as a person. Thus, it is perfectly acceptable for anyone to criticize the boss - but this concept is not a part of the Indian system. So from time to time, it is important for an organization's chief executive to get a report on the psychological health of the firm. How do people in the team feel? Are they stable? Confident? Secure? Comfortable? These are the key elements of a team's success.

In India you find that bosses kick the people below them, and butter up the people above. It should be exactly the opposite – butter up the people below, and do not be afraid to kick those at the top. For a boss to be comfortable accepting criticism from subordinates, he must feel good about himself. Self-esteem is a key prerequisite to such a system being successful.

Mental vs. Physical Workers

Here is a personal story that will bring out another serious problem facing India – the dichotomy and difference in respectability between physical and mental workers that seriously affects team performance. I had a driver named Bhumi Ram, who I thought was one of the best drivers in the world. He used to open the door for me whenever I entered or exited the car. Right in the first few days I told him, "Bhumi Ram bhai, you are not going to open the door for me. You can do that if I lose my hands." He almost started crying. He said, "Sir, what are you saying? This is my job!" I told him that I did not want him to feel like a mere driver. He had to become a team player. I told him that whenever he was not driving, he should come into my office and help out with office work – make copies, file papers, send faxes, answer phone calls or simply read - rather than sit in the car and wait for me to show up. Diversifying tasks increases workers' self-esteem and motivation and makes them a team player. Now, even if I call him for work in the middle of the night, he is ready – because I respect him for what he does.

Team Interactions

Unfortunately, when good teams do get created, they almost invariably fall apart. In the '80s, there was a great political team consisting of Rajiv Gandhi, Arun Nehru, V.P. Singh, Arun Singh and others. If that team had remained intact, India would have been a different country today. They were all the same age, were good friends, and had backgrounds outside of politics. But the team self-destructed. They developed conflicts and could not resolve them – and the nation paid the price. In our system today it is very difficult to build teams because nobody wants to be seen playing second fiddle.

It is very hard in India to find good losers. Well, you win some and you lose some. If you lose some, you should move on. You do not need to spend all your time and energy attacking the winner. You try harder, and perhaps next time you will win.

In India we have people of different cultural backgrounds, religions, ethnicities and caste groups – a fertile ground for diversity in the workplace. We should actually be experts in working with diversity. But it can only happen when we get rid of personal, caste and community interests.

It all changes when we are in America. Here, we are a small part of a much bigger scene. We are willing to compromise and accept differences because we ourselves are different. In America, we act as the minority. In India, we act as the majority – and we never think about how the minority feels in that environment.

In the United States, you become part of the team very easily, helped by a general environment that encourages teamwork. People appreciate good work and pat you on the back; your boss is open and does not mind criticism – you can tell her that she is not right and she may agree with you, and she may tell you that you have a good idea. The young are respected; there is no hierarchical system. There could be a 40-year-old CEO with a 55-year-old VP. It has nothing to do with age, instead; capability and expertise are what counts. But you do not yet see these attitudes taking hold in India.

Managers in American corporate environments who work with Indians – and perhaps even with Asians in general – need to recognize that these individuals have a tendency to feel they are not getting the recognition they deserve, or are not being respected. It must be realized that these individuals may possess a lower sense of self-esteem to begin with and therefore have to be pampered and encouraged a little more because they need it. This makes them feel better and work better.

No Substitute for Teamwork

Teamwork is key to corporate and national governance, and to accomplishing goals. The fundamental issues are respect for others, openness, honesty, communication, a willingness to disagree, the ability to resolve conflict and recognition that the larger goals of the team as a whole triumph over individual or personal agendas.

■

NEW BLOOD MAKES A MARK

Enterprise in India has traditionally been linked to family, with sons and grandsons - competent or not - heading businesses. India's true entrepreneurial spirit is now emerging in the area of technology.

In many ways, it is refreshing to see the rebirth of the entrepreneurial spirit in India, thanks to technology. A new breed of entrepreneurs is now breaking old barriers and setting up new parameters of success, infusing a new attitude and value system into age-old systems. What makes this change momentous is the fact that these young people are successful by virtue of their education and talent rather than their connections or blood. Because technology is a business based on knowledge, it is a business where only merit counts, where respect for others outside of the family becomes critical, where sharing gets you the best rewards, and where working as a team is crucial.

I think it is critical that we realize that this is a change for the better. The traditional family model that has dominated India is by its very nature contrary to the spirit of entrepreneurship and innovation. Wherever families rule, there is an inherent reluctance to bring in outside talent, probably to avoid sharing family wealth and prestige. Rather than become instruments of change and development, for years the motto of such enterprises in India remained "keeping money within the family." This attitude has kept the door to future innovation firmly shut, which has had a negative impact on the whole country in the long run.

Against this background, we have to consider if technology-driven enterprises can replace "License Raj." In many ways, the answer is yes. With globalization, liberalization and privatization, the whole perception of the country is beginning to change. Only the best can survive now as Indian companies are competing with the best players in the international arena. There are no short cuts to success anymore and technology is playing a key role in the transformation.

Value Systems

We have to remember that entrepreneurship, in the final analysis, is part and parcel of a larger value system. I am a firm believer that value systems have the power to define and transform a country's economy. For Indians to compete effectively with the rest of the world on equal footing, the character of entrepreneurship has to change. The best world businesses are built on a foundation of open structures — open to people, risk, investment and new alliances.

In spite of the challenges that reside within the system, Indian entrepreneurs on the whole have done very well. But, the critical question we have to ask ourselves is: Why do Indians do better outside the country? This stresses for us the need to overhaul the system, in order to create an environment conducive to entrepreneurship and open the doors of opportunities within the country rather than drive away talented people. Our politicians have to remember that fostering a spirit of entrepreneurship is directly equivalent to creating wealth for the country. Every person who has the drive should have the opportunity to be a future Bill Gates. In the end, it is about building wealth, where the tools are the people.

However, even in this arena, we are facing the same problems as we do with all India-related industries — India is not looking inward; our focus is to export software services rather than build technology to strengthen the nation's backbone. We aim to become a "super outsourcing resource" rather than a technology superpower. For once, we have the opportunity to look within and rework our image to the rest of the world. We want the world to look to India for its entrepreneurs, not its exports.

Now is the time for Indian entrepreneurs to build companies that will shape our future for years to come. I believe the solution to India's problems resides in giving free rein to entrepreneurs to build companies that will change the country in a fundamental way. Technology can solve India's problems. But to make this happen, we must make sure we provide the fertile ground for this change to take root. Laws need to change, processes must be refined, attitudes should be transformed, and hierarchies must make way for egalitarianism.

■

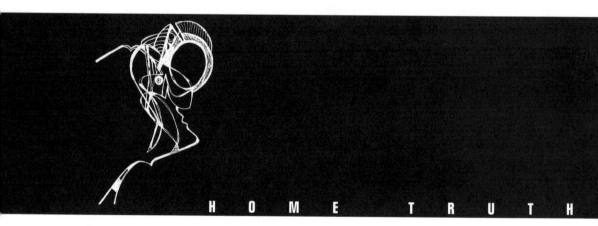

H O M E   T R U T H

| *Setting up shop in India is an arduous task, but a smart executive should relish the challeng*

I rrespective of what anyone may say about the difficulties of setting up shop and working in India, I would strongly urge anyone who has such an opportunity to grab it. Do not shy away from a great experience; there is a lot you can learn. You and India will be changed by the experience.

Everything about India is different. Perceptions, markets, considerations and outlooks, among other things, are vastly different. What makes sense in America is not necessarily the right thing to do in India. The bottom line: You cannot afford to go to India with the same bag of tricks you use in America.

Here are some key things to remember that may help one succeed.

You are Different

Looking at you, people in India may consider you one of them. But in truth, you only look like an Indian — you do not act like one. You were probably born and raised in America or another foreign land; most, if not all, of your work has been in Western countries. As a result, you are a different human being when it comes to work. It is important to recognize this difference.

The Bureaucracy Trap

Everyone has heard and read about the huge bureaucracy in India. Although India has liberalized a number of its regulations, a lot of controls and procedures remain. The key is to not worry about these things, which are mostly routine processes that everyone has to go through. Do not feel trapped by these processes and fall into fruitless criticizing or complaining. Associated with this bureaucracy is corruption and bribery. I spent ten years in India and can tell you that one can work around the system without ever offering bribes. You can be completely honest and also get things done. It may cause minor delays, but you can still achieve your goals. Besides, once you start offering bribes, there is no end to what might be demanded of you.

Different Work Environment

The work culture, work ethic and working environment are very different in India than what you have been used to. You will find that offices do not look like they do in the United States. Neither do factories. You will wonder why people are not on time and why things never work according to schedule.

Lack of Systems

In America, workflow systems and processes are in place so that even mediocre people can work efficiently. In India, no such systems exist. This can be frustrating, especially when it comes to small things that we tend to take for granted. You may have to set up many of the systems in order to create efficiencies. So be prepared to do that.

Efficiency, Quality, Time and Management

These qualities all have different meanings in India. Do not compare them with what you are used to. If you do so, you are almost certain to heighten your frustration and stress level. What you have to recognize is this – there are things that you can change and there are things that you cannot change; there are things that are in your control and there are those that are not.

Split-Level Consciousness

Employees at work will tell you what you (or the management) want to hear as opposed to what the facts are. So do not accept what people say at face value. In the United States, when people say, "I will get it done," they mean it — and chances are, they will do it. A wise manager would not immediately believe the same statement when uttered in India.

Leftover Hierarchical and Feudal Systems

Systems and structures are still hierarchical and feudal in India. That is, who you know is more important than what you know. Consequently, name-dropping is quite common. People try to establish themselves first by establishing their contacts. There are now a lot of young business executives, especially in the Information Technology industry, but they still cannot make a sufficient enough impact because people in power are still senior. It is important to recognize the age barrier that exists.

Appearances Are Not What They Seem

Don't judge people by their looks or grooming. There are some very simple-looking people in India that run multimillion-dollar businesses. In many companies, there are line-level managers in front that are outgoing and have sharp communication skills. And then there are back-office personnel, the real doers. These executives call the shots and form the brains trust. They may not have degrees from foreign universities, but their analytical skills are highly sophisticated and they have a head for numbers. Besides, they understand local issues and local markets. One should learn to recognize and respect this talent.

If you understand the above points, it will be easier to get started. India is a huge, rapidly growing economy. We all know that India is a big market. It maybe difficult to crack, but the numbers are really significant. Even if a small percentage has the capacity to buy, this is still as large as Europe. Many have more purchasing power than they have access to goods and services. And even though the system is very cost conscious, there are a lot of people who are beginning to demand quality. Automobiles are a good example: India first had Ambassadors, then Marutis, and now a host of international cars. The push for quality has completely changed the auto industry.

With the success of nonresident Indians, especially those in Silicon Valley, interfaces between Indians in the United States and Indians in India have increased substantially.

India has opened up to the world and the world has opened up to India. Many Indians and non-Indians travel back of forth doing business and spending personal time between the two countries. This trend is healthy for both countries, and these trendsetters are the real ambassadors.

■

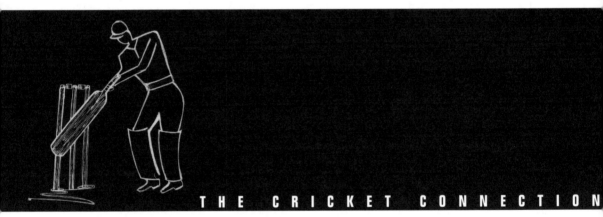

THE CRICKET CONNECTION

More than just a game, cricket and the way India plays cricket can teach us a lot of lessons in management, leadership, building a business, and ultimately, in building a nation.

For 38 days, with more than 42 games, the cricket World Cup held in 1999 in the United Kingdom galvanized the entire cricket-playing world. In India, for example, during the matches played by the Indian team, little work got done – people were hooked to their TVs, and there were few issues larger than the outcome of those matches. In London, hundreds of India supporters watched with high hopes and dreams for India to win the title. Filled with high expectations, fans brandished paraphernalia like drums and flags to express their emotions for the home team.

Play Ball

I had a rare free day during the World Cup, which gave me a chance to watch and "think through" a full game of cricket. It was between India and Zimbabwe. It was incredible to see how new television broadcast technologies were integrated into the game of cricket – charts, graphs, and strategically placed cameras that generated breathtaking replays. Given the strengths of other teams such as Australia, Pakistan and South Africa, it was clear that India faced a tough challenge to rise to the top. At the same time, I did expect them to win the game against Zimbabwe. But to my great chagrin, they lost, and I took away from it several observations that I would like to share. These observations may not be very critical, but I think they convey the connection between the way people in India play cricket, and approach work projects.

India has some very talented cricketers, like Sachin Tendulkar and Rahul Dravid. The way these two players were hitting the ball was of the first order – the precision and the timing was almost like that of a machine. But the few great performances by exceptional players were incomparable to the overall performance of the team. When you look at the Indian team, comprised of 11 individuals, you realize that somehow, the sum does not seem to add up to 11. Very high peaks, and very low averages – that's the problem I saw with the Indian cricket team, and that's the problem I see with India as a whole. Individually we may be great – but collectively our performance is poor. Averages take a lot of time and training to build up, but high averages, not peak performances, result in consistent victories.

Killer Instinct

Do you need killer instinct to play cricket? Many will argue that you don't. But I think it's important and connects directly with our very own 'chalta hai' culture, where there is a tendency to say, "We'll see," or "Well, it will get done, sometime" with every job, big or small. It is the root cause of the lack of quality of work in India. The Indian cricket team had not made up its mind on the field that it was going to do its best to win the game against Zimbabwe. The message communicated by the players' body language was, "If we win then that's great; if we don't, then that's okay too." The high-voltage energy and killer instinct you would expect to see in a team that really wanted to win was missing.

The Hierarchy of Sport

I also saw a great deal of difference in what I call the "Sudra" play and the "Brahminian" play. By *Sudra* play I mean throwing yourself into the fielding and doing anything you can to save a run. *Brahminian* play means standing around lethargically, considering fielding an unworthy cause, or thinking that the glory of the game lies only in batting and hitting fours and sixes. In reality, extra efforts, made on a collective basis, result in wins. But as far as the Indian team was concerned, this was a lost cause.

During the game, players on the Indian team did not make much of an effort in their fielding – to dive for the ball and save it from crossing the boundary. This has clear parallels with life and society in India, where traditionally, only office jobs carry respect. Most other work is considered worthless. Even in cricket there is a hierarchical mindset that is reflected in the way the team plays the game. The players need to go beyond their individual agendas – "*I* will make 100 runs," or "*I* will take 5 wickets." The goal is for the team to win, and that should remain the focus.

Time Out

During the game, I noticed that there was very little review on the field. This is very different from American football, or the American style of management for that matter, where "time out" is the signal to rethink, realign, reposition, and re-strategize based on what's happening on the field at one particular time. I didn't ever see the Indian cricket team getting together on the field to do that. This again reflects our way of conducting business. Indians tend to do very little to review and realign when working on an assignment. That's not part of our culture. Instead we rely on "karma" – the idea that fate is already decided. Self-evaluation is important, for both cricket players and for managers.

Rising to the Occasion

One of the responsibilities of a leader, whether in cricket or in management, is to set expectations for the team and to generate the enthusiasm that will motivate the team to win, to accomplish its goals. During the World Cup, it seemed that the Indian cricket team had no idea what people were expecting of them. Perhaps they were unaware that a whole nation was counting on them, was backing them and that it was the team's responsibility to take the energy of those people and win that game. Maybe they did not understand the costs of losing the game –lost time and lost productivity due to ensuing national depression. This is what happens in management of an organization as well. If the leadership is not there to motivate the team and set the stakes for the players, the team loses momentum and does not get the job done.

In watching the cricket game I realized that these are challenges of management. The skills are there, but we fail time and time again in organizing our skills, managing our resources, reviewing our agenda, and putting in the energy that is needed. I have seen this many times in India where there may be very well-laid plans for projects but the plans are not implemented because the right kind of management is not backing them up.

Organizational success or failure can almost always be traced to management. Cricket is no exception. The eleven players, chosen for a national team out of a huge cricket-loving country, must be managed by someone who can ignite killer instinct. When managers develop a business strategy, they too need to feel the energy of the teeming millions and then go into the game to win. That is the challenge.

It's possible that I read too much into that cricket game. Maybe it's no big deal — lose today, win tomorrow. But I didn't see it that way. I saw it as a reflection of what India is all about. There are vast differences in the physical sizes of India and Zimbabwe and their populations. But the differences melted on the field that day. If the Indian team lacked velocity by itself, the mass of the huge nation backing it up could have been expected to help generate greater momentum. It did not happen. We need to focus on improving management, motivating team players, generating energy. We need to go into each day saying, "How do we win? How do we change the attitude? How do we reposition ourselves?" Teams in India, whether in cricket or in business, have to do these things if they want to go out there and win.

■

TACKLING NATURAL DISASTERS IN INDIA

In recent years, India has seen its fair share of natural disasters, climaxing in the devastating earthquake in Gujarat. What can be done to control huge losses from such disasters? Policy, technology and management are the three fundamental elements of an effective disaster management system.

India is a densely populated country, with a large percentage of its people poor and served by an underdeveloped and inadequate infrastructure. This results in a higher rate of devastation from natural disasters, as we have seen in Gujarat. Technology can play a major role in controlling the loss of life and property at these times. But without proper policy support and management skills, technology is ineffective.

Policy

India needs a national agency — akin to the U.S. Federal Emergency Management Administration (FEMA) — to focus exclusively on disaster management. Currently, the Ministry of Agriculture oversees disaster response, though it lacks expertise! At the same time, the states need systems to implement the policies and procedures put forth by the national agency. There's nothing new in these ideas — we have always known these things. Yet nothing has really been done about it. Until we get some kind of synchronized policy framework at the national, state and district levels and focus on coordination, communication and management, no amount of technology will help.

Technology

In disasters like the Gujarat quake, the first 100 hours are the most crucial for saving lives. Every minute matters. After the quake struck, telecommunications links were down for more than two days. People lay buried alive for days. Later, as aid reached the affected areas, truckloads of emergency supplies reportedly waited at the airport for several days, paralyzed by confusion over how to get life-saving materials to the injured. Volunteers who arrived at the disaster site were not properly coordinated. Look carefully at these circumstances and you'll see that two areas of infrastructure technology were needed: access and databases. (We are not discussing technologies for removal of debris, and so on. That is a separate discussion, beyond the purview of this chapter).

When disaster strikes, reestablishing telecommunication links with the affected areas is crucial to effectively use available resources and disseminate ground information to the rest of the world. People want to know what happened to family members, friends, businesses and property. It is also critical to know how many are dead or hurt, how many are in the hospital, how many doctors are on duty, what the conditions are at treatment facilities, and what resources are needed. This is entirely a communication issue.

Modular mobile wireless exchanges are the workable answer. They can be flown into the affected areas within two hours of the disaster. These satellite-based systems, used only in disaster conditions, would have backup battery power, so the units work even when there is no electricity. Depending on the location and scope of the disaster, the exchanges could support voice, fax, videoconferencing, e-mail and Internet access.

In contrast to this, authorities in Gujarat attempted to fix existing communications systems that had already been destroyed! That always takes a long time. What is needed is a temporary overlay system that doesn't require existing working infrastructure. These systems exist today, and wireless technologies are the most effective in these situations.

Databases

Access technologies will depend on existing databases with detailed information pertaining to specific physical areas. These databases will include vital statistics such as: medical resources available in the area; local transportation that can be pooled and deployed rapidly for help: detailed maps; weather information; terrain; the impact of similar disasters in the past in the same area; the kinds of clothing effective in the area; profile of population density in the area; and the locations of schools, nursing homes. All of this has to be prearranged and recorded in massive databanks, for every part of the country. It must be instantly accessible by relief agencies in times of crisis. In Gujarat, alas, nothing of this sort was available. Everything was ad hoc, chaotic. This reduced the effectiveness of relief efforts a great deal.

Remote sensing satellite technology can be used very effectively to collect physical terrain data. All database resources have to be integrated with the newly designed disaster management systems. At the same time, it is crucial to develop dynamic databases of information to be collected during the disaster relief operations. These could be mined by software programs to effectively streamline relief efforts. That would provide a better picture of the resources needed in each area and how to get them there.

Today, global positioning systems in cars are able to pinpoint a location within five to ten meters. Using the same technology, we should be able to scan the area of an earthquake by satellite. By comparing existing databases to the new information, authorities would be able to pinpoint high impact areas. People walking around the entire area were doing all of this manually in Gujarat. Somebody should have been looking at this on a screen!

Management

Once policies and technology are in place, questions remain: How do you manage disaster relief? Who provides leadership? Management systems must be built on expertise, communication and coordination. Team structures at the national, state, district and village/city level have to be predefined.

The government has to be the most involved in this area. Recently, the government of India established a committee of five secretaries to investigate the earthquake! Neither volunteer groups nor NGOs were appointed to serve the panel. The secretaries have no expertise in disaster response, and thus they obviously can't get the job done. As a result, India's disaster preparedness will never improve.

Training in all of these facets of disaster management cannot be undermined. Potential relief personnel have to be put through drills, akin to fire drills. In crisis situations, the general public gets very emotional. Relief staff should have the interpersonal skills to manage this. There must also be total media and public relations management during these times. That, too, requires proper training.

The Gujarat earthquake has really stirred everybody up in India. Although people are now talking about disaster management systems, they tend to forget things over time. Unfortunately the quake was such a major blow that it will be hard to forget. I hope something will get done. Several initiatives need to be taken, but in India the leadership does not think in a constructive manner.

I assure you, if 100 smart people get to work on this, in six months India will have the best disaster management system in the world. Standards are available and there has been a lot of international discussion and experience. India needs to tap into the resources that many foreign organizations have offered.

Individually, people at a personal level are doing their best and helping everybody. They're going beyond their caste and religious boundaries. With leveled buildings, the society itself was leveled. All of this now needs top-down management and leadership to create effective disaster management systems, driven by technologies available today.

| *The Telecom Infrastructure: Past, present and future.*

The process of modernizing the telecom sector started in the Rajiv Gandhi era. The very first task was to separate the postal service from telecom – they were integrated and had combined assets. This separation took almost three years – and even after that, a lot of things were left unsorted.

Then, the digitization of telecom was initiated. Until then, the entire telephone network was analog.

Thereafter, C-DoT (Center for the Development of Telematics) was launched as an indigenous telecom development center to develop our own products and services with an emphasis on rural communication (The complete C-DoT story is in the next chapter). The plan was to connect all of the district headquarters through direct trunk dialing – building a network throughout the country – including fiber-optic links between Calcutta, Bombay, Delhi and Madras. Then the uncovered rural areas were to be penetrated, to install exchanges and provide services. The Western model of increasing density doesn't work in most developing countries. The key here is access to the telephone.

Simultaneously, there was experimentation with the corporatization of the Department of Telecom, with the formation of two companies – Videsh Sanchar Nigam Ltd. (VSNL) and Mahanagar Telephone Nigam Ltd. (MTNL). Though the companies were separate, labor remained a big problem. The total telecom labor force was about 500,000, which came to a shocking 100 people for every 1,000 lines. The labor unions would not let us reduce this number. Eventually it was decided that there would be no more recruitment, and that the number of lines would be quadrupled.

Privatization

Then began the process of privatization and deregulation. The first phase was to deregulate and privatize the production of telephone, switching and transmission equipment. This took almost five years. Now India is in a position to produce almost all the equipment locally — some of it using local technology, designed and produced at C-DoT, and the rest using technology from multinational companies like Siemens, Motorola, Fujitsu, Ericsson, NEC and AT&T.

The second phase was to privatize the value-added services, like voice, data, and video conferencing. In this phase, the key element was privatizing cellular services. Licenses were issued to two operators for cellular services in each major city. There was no license fee for cellular services, so a lot of private parties saw it as lucrative and entered the business.

The third phase was to privatize basic telecom services. But when the licenses for the basic services were issued, it turned out that companies had bid too high in most regions. The local partners were not able to come up with the capital to get the license. So only a few companies actually have licenses for basic services today. They have started basic telecom services in competition with the Department of Telecom. That is, in states like Madhya Pradesh, Gujarat and Maharashtra, for example, there is DoT and a second, private operator. In other places, either people were looking for capital, or nobody came through – either because people thought that these states were not worth bidding for, or because their bids were lower than the government's expectations.

Thus, basic-service privatization didn't go well. It is now stuck in a vicious circle where a lot of licenses are issued, but no financing is available. Most of the private companies in the telecom business in India are big family business groups with no experience in telecom. They just decided to club with the big international operators. But these international operators themselves are busy guarding their home turf, since they are faced with competition and the changing complexion of the industry, which includes the integration of voice, data and video. Consequently, these companies are not too interested in going all the way to India to put in capital. So the expectation that privatization would bring large investments from outside India has not really materialized.

The problem is further aggravated by the fact that the private operators, who are obviously profit-oriented, are attracted to high-usage customers. The world over, 20 percent of the customers generate 80 percent of the revenues. But it is the remaining 80 percent who really need the phones! The situation is aggravated by the government's high license fees, which make the operators gravitate toward high-usage customers. This misguided policy was designed to boost government revenues, while the real need was for incentives for private operators to add lines, providing services to people who need the phones.

And that brings us to the main issue: The new telecom policy released by the government in May of 1994 envisioned that by the end of 1997, every village in the country would have a telephone. Today, more than 300,000 villages in India still do not have a telephone.

Telecom Commission

In the process of speeding telecom penetration in the country, we started the

Telecom Commission during the Rajiv Gandhi administration. The idea was to give autonomy to a group of professionals to drive the telecom business. Unfortunately the Telecom Commission got caught in controversy, and as a result has not been able to make bold decisions to move forward. It still has to go through ministers, secretaries and all other bureaucratic bottlenecks for every decision. India could have done a lot more in telecom. It should have had 20 million lines by now, aiming for 35 million lines by the year 2000.

In the early days, we focused more on accessibility and installed many public call offices all over the country. Simultaneously, we also implemented the Direct Distance Dialing (DDD) service throughout the country, eliminating 50,000 operators who used to handle manual calls. This way, almost all districts and taluks were connected with each other. Internationally, India is now connected to almost 200 countries. But this is nowhere near sufficient: India still has about 13 million lines, but needs at least 50 million.

With the existing Indian conditions, it costs about $1,000 for a phone line to be set up in a new location. Thus, we are talking about a total investment of $37 billion. Where is this money going to come from? A $1 billion investment in telecom can effectively be funded by $250 million of equity, $250 million of debt and $500 million from the operations of the business. This is the kind of proposal that the government must entertain. There should be policies that are clear and geared toward growth and not control.

The problem is that the people in the Telecom Commission who have the power to make these policies, are afraid of court cases and accusations of favoritism and corruption. Somebody has to be gutsy and say: "You can scrutinize me, you can put me in jail, but this is what has to be done. So let's do it."

Indigenous Production

India had developed a large manufacturing base of telecom equipment – both indigenous and that developed by international companies. This base has been all but killed, because the plants have no orders! The governmental systems are not set up to plan ahead. Orders for 1998 will be given in 1998 itself, when ideally, orders in this industry should be placed two years in advance so that the manufacturer can plan production.

Thus, the antiquated management system is trying to cope with modern technology. And frankly, I don't see this changing too soon. The lack of a strong government in recent years has further delayed decision-making.

Stumbling Blocks

One major factor that is stifling the rapid development of telecom in India today is lack of investment from the private sector. But that will only come if the projects are viable. Let's say a company gets a license in state A, for which the government asks for an initial fee of Rs. 5 billion over a set period of time. Add to that the equipment and other costs, and the total cost becomes so high that the project is no longer viable — for either the companies or the Indian and foreign institutional investors.

So unless the government makes some concessions: reduce the license fees, give tax relief, or other incentives, these projects are not going to take off in a big way.

Long Distance View

Telecom in India is at a very critical juncture today. Unless some key, bold decisions are made, the needs of the people will not be met. China, for example, is adding 15 million new lines every year – that's like creating one NYNEX (before its merger with Bell Atlantic) every year! They have simply put a few hundred thousand military personnel to work, digging and laying out cable – and that's how they get things done! By 2007, China will have two-thirds of the world's telephones. That's the kind of growth we need in India.

For this, we need clarity of policy. The basic telephony privatization projects should become viable. Since the investments required are very large, they should be sought from the right sources. If the investors don't feel comfortable, these projects are obviously not going to get off the ground.

India can't afford to grow at the "Indian rate of growth" in telecom. In India, to touch the roof, you have to aim at the moon — and even then, you barely touch the roof. If we plan to add 10 million lines, maybe we will add seven. But if we say that we will only add 2 million, we will not do even that many.

We are a country of a billion people. But we don't think like a billion people; we think like a Banana Republic. If we cannot have the velocity, at least we can, and should, have momentum!

■

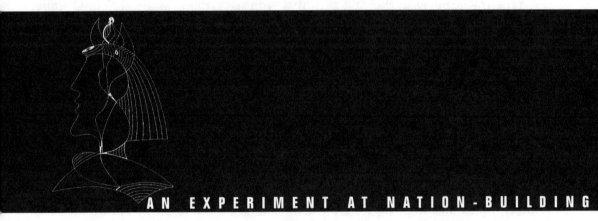

AN EXPERIMENT AT NATION-BUILDING

The reason it's important to talk about C-DoT today is that the current IT fervor in India has some of its roots in the C-DoT experience started in the early '80s.

W e often forget that the current multi-billion dollar Indian high-tech industry began with some early modernizing experiments that set the pace for growth. C-DoT was one of the first to emerge from those experiments. C-DoT, or the Center of Development for Telematics, was set up in 1984 by Mrs. Indira Gandhi's government, under the Ministry of Communication. Despite the fact that it was a Government of India enterprise, it was conceived as an autonomous body, vested with full authority and flexibility to develop state-of-the-art telecommunication technology to meet the needs of the Indian telecommunication network. The key objective was to build a center for excellence in the area of telecom technology. It started as a research project aimed at the indigenous development of digital switching systems (telephone hardware and software); what began as a telecom research center became C-DoT with a mandate to produce (initially) switching and (later) transmission systems suitable for Indian conditions.

Even though I was behind the conception of the idea, there was no way I could have done it without the government backing it every step of the way. First Indira Gandhi, then her son Rajiv, made it possible. Rajiv had the vision to take the country to the 21st century, even back then. Many ridiculed Rajiv for his ideas, as they were clearly ahead of their time. He saw technology as the entry point to solving India's problems. Indeed, it is his attempt at modernization that has made India what it is; his vision and initiative set the ball rolling in India. As a country, we could have gone way further had he been re-elected. He may have made mistakes — but he learned from them. Who doesn't make mistakes? His commitment to nation building was a hundred percent.

What made Rajiv indispensable to the C-DoT experiment was that he was totally committed to technological advancement and modernization. Once he saw the potential and need for C-DoT, he gave me carte blanche to bring in all the changes that were needed. He always took an interest in what transpired, and was always there to give that pat on the back. Once, after finishing a very challenging project, I invited Rajiv to meet the team. His visit meant a great deal to each team member — after shaking his hand, one young guy did not wash his hand for 30 days!

Attitude and Motivation

I conceived of C-DoT as a company with a different attitude and a different spirit. We decided to cut through the bureaucracy and create a new work ethic — a work culture that was totally foreign to the country. Therefore, I started

C-DoT with young people in their 20's. The work environment we created within C-DoT was totally different from that of any company in India: I aspired to shield these motivated young people from the rigors of day-to-day work pressures in India, and in return they gave C-DoT their best and made it what it is today. At C-DoT, there were no hierarchies, and there was total emphasis on merit. Employees were inspired and motivated to perform their best, and we gave them the sense that they were contributing to nation building.

From the beginning, C-DoT marched to its own drum-beat. When I dispatched a secretary to fly with some papers to Bangalore, some bureaucrats raised a furor. "She should be sent by third class," they said. "How dare you send a secretary by air!" My response: "I don't give a damn. What gets work done fastest is the best way." I think of it as a company that has its foundation in innovation and enterprise, which is why the core team of 300 or 400 people has all moved on to other ambitious independent projects in Silicon Valley, in Bangalore, and in Mumbai. That tells us that the experiment worked — more than simply picking the right people for the right job, we were creating people devoted to innovation.

When I look back today, I consider it a very challenging project. We set goals for ourselves that were very demanding. At that time, who would have thought of exchanges in rural areas? Or a public call office with long-distance and international direct-dial facilities on every street? Although many believed that these things were just not possible, we were devoted to our goals. Our motto was, "One rural exchange a day." We took telecom to the villages, building products that would withstand the dust, heat and other infrastructure problems unique to India.

The resistance to the idea was tremendous. Everyday we heard the "can't do" slogans from our critics. In many ways, the ignorance of our young employees was a blessing — as they did not believe in the "can't do" attitude. We went forward, installing 36 million connections in 36 months.

End Game

The downslide came after Rajiv was out of power. Until then, we had excellent backing and could bring in whatever innovations we thought necessary. After him, we were abused, humiliated and slandered. But if you are focused and driven, no one can touch you — and C-DoT proved that to people. Now it is a 15-year-old company with over 1,500 employees. We built everything from scratch. We were successful in most of what we had sought out to achieve.

More than 50 to 60 percent of Indian telecom is built on C-DoT products and, despite their high quality, C-DoT products are cheaper than those of multinationals.

My days with C-DoT are over for good: I never think of returning to them. I have other commitments now, and the younger people are more suited for that role. The moral of the C-DoT experiment is this: Even in India, you can do what you want. Initiative, discipline, drive and creating the right work environment are all you need.

■

CHANGING IT FOCUS: FROM INDUSTRY TO PEOPLE

The Government of India has taken several initiatives to enable the Indian IT industry to achieve higher results, including the formation of a national IT Task Force, composed of leading government officials and IT industry authorities. Though certainly a great step forward for India's approach towards information technology, it reveals a critical lacuna in its conceptualization. Is it IT for the IT industry's sake, or IT for the people?

In today's world the boundaries between telecom, television, broadband, hardware and software are merging. Previously, telephone was on wire and television was on air. Now telephone is on the air and television is on the wire. The other day I saw a cartoon, which said, 'Honey, will you answer the television, I am watching the telephone'. That summarizes where we are.

The Need for IT

As a social leveler, information technology ranks second only to death. It can raze cultural barriers, overwhelm economic inequalities and even compensate for intellectual disparities. In short, technology can put unequal human beings on an equal footing, and that makes it the most potent democratizing tool ever devised.

But this whole information revolution has not been clearly understood by people in India. They think they are somehow not going to be affected by it. But I think we are going to be severely affected by it.

India, like most of the Third World, has been using its priceless foreign exchange to buy the West's abandoned technology and install obsolete equipment that doomed the country to move like a telecom snail while Europe, America and Japan were beginning to move like information greyhounds. The technological disparity was becoming greater not smaller. India and countries like her were falling farther and farther behind not just in the ability to chat with relatives or call the doctor but, much more critically, in the capacity to coordinate development activities, pursue scientific study, conduct business, operate markets and participate more fully in the international community.

Thus, there are two reasons for needing telecommunications and other information technologies: not only can they help Indians create wealth in every walk of life, they can also create wealth of its own. Unless we have both, we have no future as a nation.

IT plays an indispensable role in promoting openness, accessibility, accountability, connectivity, democracy and decentralization - all the 'soft' qualities so essential for effective social, economic, and political development. India needs the capacity to network with people, ideas and initiatives. This is as critical and fundamental to nation building as water, agriculture, health and housing, and without it, India's democracy could founder.

New Developments

The present BJP government in India should be complimented for taking this initiative on IT and congratulated on the speed with which they have been able to set up the national IT Task Force, and publish their recommendations. Such a great change normally does not happen so quickly in India. The impetus for the Task Force came from several people, including Chandrababu Naidu, the Chief Minister of Andhra Pradesh, who has been the driving force for IT industry in the state. He has created a sense of urgency, and, to some extent, a competitive environment with various other neighboring states to implement IT in the government. Besides Mr. Naidu, many other professionals, scientists, industry groups, and others have contributed to this effort.

This recommendation document reflects the basic implementation plan, delving into details such as duty for hardware, software export, facilities and the need for concessions and incentives. In my opinion, however, the document responds to the pressures of the various industry groups more than it creates a vision to solve people's problems in India. Though a good document that represents a step forward, it perhaps should have been issued after a vision document.

But, before we go into that, let's not forget that it was really Rajiv Gandhi who ushered India into the Information Age. Many of today's champions of IT then labeled him an elitist, and criticized him for not being in touch with reality. He was the first to emphasize new policies for electronics, software, telecom and other emerging technologies. Truly concerned about the application of IT, he catalyzed the computerization of railway reservation, creation of technology missions, computerization of land records and the activities of the Planning Commission. We made a lot of progress by computerizing a number of government processes, creating the National Informatics Center, C-DoT (Centre for Development of Telematics) and CDAC (Centre for Development of Advanced Computing), among other institutions. It was during his time also that we started inviting global multinational companies such as GE, Texas Instruments and Hewlett Packard to do their software work in India.

We now need to focus on an IT vision for the 21st century. I am not criticizing what has been done. However, the 108-point program introduced in 2000 on IT policy is no silver bullet for a nation as complex as India. Based on a recent opportunity to work on similar issues in some other countries, I broadly recommend focusing on five key aspects: Creating IT awareness in order to create IT leaders; promoting IT in government and administration; taking IT to the people; developing IT infrastructures; and train the people to take IT to the limit.

Creating IT Awareness

A need for IT applications and benefits among the people has to be generated in a country like India. It is often said India has science, but no "scientific temper". As far as IT is concerned, India has IT, but no IT culture - it lacks the ability to organize, process, understand and share information. These skills require a different mindset and the creation of a new work culture, which can only be developed when a majority of people understand the importance of IT. This IT awareness can be created through TV programs, conferences, seminars, committees, presentations, exhibitions and other public events. This way, a large number of people — not only the elite — can relate to IT and associated benefits.

Promoting IT in Government

At the central, state and district levels, the focus must be on the things that the governments can begin to implement to improve public service. I have been told that some states have 20,000 forms for the public. Whether it has to do with pension, admission in universities or getting ration cards - all of these forms need to be simplified, standardized, reduced in number and then fed into computers. This is also a great opportunity to examine all our existing processes, to regard how we have been doing things in the past and use IT to change how we will be doing it in the future. The legal system is a classic example: We have millions of cases pending in our courts. How can IT help rid us of bottlenecks in the legal system? Similarly, finance, urban development, health, transport, industry, education could be vastly improved if we can learn to think differently, and to think IT.

Taking IT to the People

Chandrababu Naidu plans to focus on IT in government and find ways to make his administration more efficient, productive and systematic. This should be done by every state. However, we need to go beyond this and take IT to the people and not just leave it with the government. We can do that through distance learning, community centers, tele-medicine, e-commerce, electronic cash, virtual universities, employment, housing, rentals, and sales - and then relate IT to basic human needs. Today, if I wanted to test the quality of my village's water, I wouldn't know where to go. Water testing laboratories exist, but who knows where? IT can solve this problem - using latest software, searchable databases can be created with all this information and put on the

Internet. These small solutions will bring IT closer to the people. They'll be able to get on the Internet to find information - the nearest hospitals, the latest prices for agricultural produce, how to grow better tomatoes, how to repair the water pump -all simple little problems that nonetheless currently take a lot of time to solve.

One of the problems I faced at the technology missions was to make sure that training materials reach the people who needed them. Let's say we order 50,000 booklets on the repair of water pumps. We knew we wouldn't get all 50,000 from the printer in our hands in the first place. Then we'd have to send the booklets all over India, a massive job in itself. Finally, when the booklet reaches the village, the supervisor ends up keeping it in his or her own locker, since that is the only copy they have! Thus, despite major efforts, the information does not reach the intended recipients. The Internet, however, can effectively bypass that whole distribution system; it eclipses the need to print, package or mail. The information goes right to the people who need it, in their local language.

Developing IT Infrastructure and Business Potential

To promote IT, we must develop appropriate infrastructure - appropriate institutions and policies. We need to convene a broadcasting and regulatory framework, which is currently being implemented. A digital high-speed backbone has to be put into place that provides universal access. Intellectual property, research and development facilities and industry associations need to be considered, as well as venture capital and public market access, small business promotion and encouragement of competitive environment to create new business potential.

Develop Human Resources for IT

We are lucky to have several private institutions such as NIIT and Aptech to train thousands of young students for IT fundamentals. But if IT is to go all the way down to the masses for real applications in the future, we need to train a lot more people with vocational capabilities in software, applications, hardware and so on. The key to mastering the IT industry is human resources. This cannot be achieved simply by opening four more open universities. It's about co-op programs, industry participation and interface, research and development interface, employment incentives and scholarships. It's about constantly innovating to find new ways to get IT to the people.

For the points put forth in the IT Task Force paper to have real relevance to the future, they need to relate to one or more of these five categories. Points that specify whether, for instance, we should reduce custom duty for components worth Rs. 2000 are irrelevant to creating the real infrastructure to promote IT. Each of the points must aim at larger goals.

Unfortunately in India, most of the decisions are made in New Delhi. We need to investigate the role of Panchayat Raj system in IT policy - we can't have real decentralization without a combination of IT and Panchayat. For instance, how would you train a bunch of villagers in managing accounts, preparing a balance sheet, collecting taxes or providing services?

I wish India's IT policy would go beyond what the IT industry wants, to what IT can do for the people. And that is the real message. "What should we do to promote the IT industry?" is not the way to look at it. We need to ask instead, "How can we really use IT as a tool to solve India's problems?"

There was a time when you would go to a railway reservation center in India, stand in line 5 for an hour or more and then ask for a ticket for Bhopal, and the officer will say, "That's window 8." And you start all over again. Today, you can go to any window and buy a ticket from anywhere to anywhere — around a million people do it every day. IT benefits are real, immediate, and affect, even in this one example, a million people every day.

Once again I would like to compliment the initiative taken by the IT Task Force. But let's not lose track of the fact that IT is not for just a few people; it's not just to increase exports of software and make a few companies productive and rich. The real potential and use of IT in India is to solve problems for the masses, to empower people with instant information in their local languages.

The IT policies have been created and submitted by people in the IT industry. Now the users of IT need to get involved. Educators, doctors, administrators, and other such professionals need to suggest which needs of theirs might be solved by IT, just as doctors should recommend where IT may benefit them. The IT Task Force's goals should be based on more than a technology-action plan; they should stem from a people-action plan.

■

I N T E R N E T   A S   A   T O O L

The Internet is a golden opportunity for India. It presents a chance to revolutionize aged, slow and failing bureaucratic processes with state-of-the-art, instantaneous, productive electronic methods.

It's time to take a leap. A lot of India's antiquated and stumbling systems are standing in the way of progress. And as the rest of the world keeps becoming faster, smaller and clearer, India must get over its obsession with paper. Instead of clinging to these old ways, we should examine what the Internet, with its speed, convenience and transparency can do to reform these inefficient processes.

Sure, the Internet has been introduced in India. But the true power of the Internet doesn't lie in accessing a few remote databases or placing a couple of classified ads. The true power of the Internet lies in its ability to eliminate old and problematic ways of doing things and replace them with modern, fast-paced solutions. In order for India to capitalize on this opportunity, we must re-examine each sector of Indian life in light of the IT revolution.

Push Buttons, Not Paper!

Let's begin with the financial sector, a huge part of Indian day-to-day activity. The financial sector can be divided into two basic parts: the whole banking process, on one side, and the money/currency aspects on the other. The banking process includes everything from how your money is deposited to how funds are transferred, bills are paid, accounts are tracked, as well as the paperwork that is involved in these activities. All of these aspects must be evaluated in light of the Internet, which is capable of reforming the entire banking process.

We can begin banking reforms by creating laws that allow for digital signatures, electronic banking, wire transfers and other modern methods. All of these areas will create currency on the Internet; before long we will see less and less paper. With the introduction of electronic banking, the current Indian financial arena - from bookkeeping to check writing - will become obsolete overnight. We have to convert India's antiquated banks into high-tech, electronic, Internet banks. This will make transactions much more rapid and accessible. Users will be able to check their accounts and transfer money through their mobile phones. All of this is technologically feasible; we just need to create laws that will allow us to implement the changes.

Along with convenience and speed, one of the best things about information technology is that it creates an open and transparent system. This cuts down corruption because it exposes dubious and dodgy ways of doing things. Creating transparent systems is a social transformation that I believe will be of great value not just to India, but to all developing nations. Developing countries have created a climate in which a select few have access to privileged knowledge. We need to replace this with an open system geared toward performance and productivity. IT, with its ability to disseminate and decentralize knowledge, forces this sort of change.

Moreover, in order to take advantage of these features, the average user would not need to have a computer at home. In the last ten years, we have put in place a system of 650,000 PCOs. These can be converted into Internet kiosks and moved into local areas. By creating these public Internet terminals, we can make banking cheaper, faster and more convenient. These changes may take up to three to five years to implement, though they really shouldn't take more than two.

What's Money, Really?

The second piece, which is more challenging, is the concept of money. What is a rupee? What does it stand for, and what does it mean? Before independence, we had close to three hundred different currencies. Each state had its own money. I've seen coins from the state of Kutch, Baroda and other regions. Despite there being lots of different types of money in India, trade among states was vibrant. In fact, the idea of standardization of currency is actually quite new in India, dating back only some 60 to 70 years. This is because money is essentially a token of trust and was invented because citizens needed trust in order to exchange goods and services.

It is very difficult to find coins and small notes in India — finding change required for a billion people is no small matter. I am told India flies in thousands of tons of coins and currencies every year. We do not have the capability to print all of our currency. Due to the rigors of the Indian environment, the life cycle of the currency is notably short. Currency is damaged easily, and needs to be burned and replaced after a while. Printing or importing currency, distributing it, and, after a while, taking it out and burning it is a costly, inconvenient and unnecessary process. Electronic systems can reduce India's currency problem by converting many of our tokens of trust from paper and metal into bytes.

We could help to remedy the currency problem with the introduction of devices such as smart cards and digital wallets. If the 50 to 100 million people in India who conduct the vast majority of transactions were provided these devices, we could eliminate a significant amount of the problems of carrying cash and making change. Even if we were to charge consumers an initial sum of a few thousand rupees, these devices would justify their cost through the benefits they offer. We would be providing consumers with a lifetime device allowing them to download cash, pay phone bills, buy train tickets and perform a variety of other functions. Indians need to carefully consider the larger, long-term aspects of these solutions. By switching to a more digital system, we could significantly reduce the amount of money we need to print every year.

Money on the Move

Compare the larger benefits of moving money at electronic speeds with how it is currently moved. If money were circulating instead of sitting in the bank for two weeks at a time, it would generate more money, which would dramatically accelerate the economy. We are talking about billions of dollars moving fast. The Internet can create a tremendous amount of wealth through the restructuring of financial systems into electronic media. Along with wealth, this restructuring would also create a large number of high-tech job opportunities. Obsolete professions such as bookkeeping would be upgraded to more modern and productive occupations.

Sharing Knowledge

In 1999, I was in Ahmedabad for a conference called "Action India" to energize volunteer activities in the country. Two friends from Chicago — Prakash Desai and Shiben Ganju – joined me in organizing the event. About 200 people, including several from the United States, came for the conference that was launched from Mahatma Gandhi's Sabarmati Ashram and organized at the Indian Institute of Management.

There is so much talent inside and outside India in a variety of fields, but the two rarely meet and interact. The message we tried to send out at the conference is: The Internet is now a perfect vehicle to network and we all need to make renewed efforts to interact in a way that can make a difference to the lives of millions.

The people we met in India from various voluntary agencies have done a lot of valuable and interesting work in many different fields. These include promoting science in tribal areas, advancing women's issues all across the country, improving literacy and education and providing safe drinking water in some parts of the country.

Somehow it still appears that all this hard work has not added up to make a big difference in the lives of most people. This is partly because these projects are mostly small, and in certain cases because people are spending a lot of time in learning and educating themselves, they are not able to quickly share the knowledge with others.

Yet what appealed most to me is the enthusiasm of the people to address basic developmental issues. The desire to help was very evident in them. But also evident was a sense of frustration because they were unable to make a difference.

People are very eager to volunteer, but in many instances don't know how to contribute in a meaningful way. It's frustrating to see all this energy waiting to be tapped, and apparently no way to do so. I get the same feedback from people of Indian origin in the United States who ask, "I want to help, this is my expertise but what do I do and whom can I contact."

Unfortunately, India still has no framework for many activities. Neither are there a large number of role models. Nobody shares his or her experience with others in a way that can be meaningful. This is where I think the Net can be useful. I know that the process has already started. People are posting several new Web sites and sharing information. But most of it is happening without a basic structure. The key is to connect the volunteer agencies with others.

What is also missing is mass participation and momentum. I am sure that if a lot of the voluntary activity can be done on the Net, it would quickly multiply the number of people who will participate. If something is going on in Orissa, how can somebody in Kerala instantly participate in it without just reading a few paragraphs on the event in a newspaper? The answer lies in the Net.

The message that rings out loud and clear is this: harness the power of the Net in linking voluntary activity.

Bridging The Gap

On the one hand, there is so much to do; and on the other so many willing to do things. But unfortunately the two can't come together in fruitful association. I see a number of such gulfs in India — between the haves and have-nots; the rich and poor; educated and illiterates, to cite a few. The challenge: How to bridge the gap?

The Internet is the fastest, most efficient way to empower people. But today, the Net is still being seen as an opportunity only for computer professionals, and unfortunately, not as a tool to empower people.

It's good to build companies with large market capitalization and engage in software exports. But that is not enough to solve the larger problems of India. India's challenge is to bridge a variety of gaps that exist in its society.

Indians in high-tech around the world can help in this task. If two or three groups can get their networking teams together on certain issues, they can make a difference.

In order to fully harness the power of the Internet, we must analyze what it can do for each sector of India's day-to-day affairs. The sectors of education, finance, transport, and healthcare, to name a few, can be vastly improved and transformed by the use of these methods. We must recognize the Internet for what it is - not just another piece of technology, but a unique historical opportunity to transform old, inefficient procedures into simple, user friendly, convenient, and accessible solutions.

■

KEEP THE CONTINUITY

People of Indian origin need to maintain active contacts with India. The chain should not be broken. Their expertise will help to develop India in a rapidly changing world. Here's how the Indian diaspora can make meaningful contributions to further the development of India?

Non-Resident Indians (NRIs), having lived out of India for some time, have acquired a good background in business and technology. In the process they have also acquired the management skills needed to get things done. NRIs have developed problem-solving capabilities in a variety of fields, often in hostile and competitive environments. Thus, they have the education, experience, and, on top of that, self-confidence that comes with success and economic prosperity.

Many NRIs who are still connected with friends and family in India experience a disparity between their life in America and life back home. They want to do something to help India and constantly ask questions like, "How can I make a contribution? What do I do? What can I do?"

Where NRIs Fit In

And that's where I have an interest in linking our people in America with the people in India. There have been a lot of interesting things going on in India that Indians in India and Indians in America don't know about.

Take for example, NICNET, developed by National Informatics Center (NIC). They have been able to connect all of the district headquarters, through a computer data-link on satellite to a supercomputer in Delhi. Thus we have a massive database. Today our annual budget is prepared by NIC on computers. To make everything available as an organized database at one place is itself a major accomplishment.

Another example is the computerization of land records. It is an area as basic as computerization of railway reservation. Look at what the Center for Development of Telematics (C-DoT) has done in terms of developing software for telephone switching using Indian talent. Center for Development of Advanced Computing (C-DAC) has been developing 'Param' a whole family of supercomputers with parallel processing. The Defense Research & Development Organization (DRDO) is doing excellent work in Defense Applications. Thus, there are many government agencies doing well in developmental activities. In the private sector it is remarkable what companies like NIIT, Wipro and many others have achieved.

In the Indian situation, one has to be interested in the process as well as product. Technology may be complex, but human motivations and interactions are even more so. India has great young engineers, and I believe there is nothing they can't accomplish if we challenge them and give them a proper environment to work in.

Besides computerizing government and private sectors, another area that is of great interest to me is linking computers to social needs. For example, at the Rajiv Gandhi foundation, with the help of NIIT we have developed a software package for disabled children who cannot push keys to access computers. The knowledge of these projects would be very useful and educational for Indian professionals all over the world. It will connect them to their roots, and will motivate them to bring something useful back home.

Technology professionals of Indian origin have a major contribution to make to the country's social development. It is not just hiring some software programmers and earning some money. That's fine. I have no problem with that. But in the process there are lots of little things to be done, which connect to our roots, and I think that's where the excitement should be. There is more to this information business than business. And my interest is how do we bring about social transformation through this, whether it is in art, culture or dance, or in the mind-set, or in education of our children, or in developing new games, which have their roots in India – why can't Hanuman be as popular as Mickey Mouse?

Yes, a lot of things are being done. But the problem is that our efforts in India are in many ways mediocre. We don't have that quality of focus. In India everything is there but it is not there. Everybody knows everything but they really don't know anything. This is a country where no matter what you say, you can do exactly the opposite and get away with it. It's a land of contrasts. People may do good work in IT or multimedia, but the proof of the pudding is in sales. Can anybody claim to have sold a product in millions? If you sold five thousand, it's not worth it. It is the high volume market reach that matters. Are we really being noticed in the global market? With all the expertise, is there a single globally successful software product today that says 'Made in India'?

Let us explore some of the areas in which they can indeed make a contribution. I have identified about eight different possibilities. The first four are business and profession related and the rest relate to social contributions.

Get a Job

The first possibility, of course, is that anyone can go and work for an Indian company in India. A lot of very good companies are looking for experienced talent in technology and management. Personally, I believe that pursuing the average job may not be the most interesting and challenging way to make a contribution in India.

Work for a Multinational Company (MNC)

A lot of NRIs have preferred to go to India and work for a MNC, most often the same company that they worked for in the United States. Here they have the advantage of not being uprooted from their establishment in America and can expect to enjoy comparable benefits and facilities. But to make this work, one has to lobby around in the company to find the right kind of connection in India. Although many American companies are already established in India, many small or medium sized companies are not. Still, smaller companies may be looking for a local partner to help bring their company's technology to India through a joint venture.

Be an Entrepreneur

In India it is difficult to be an entrepreneur. This is largely due to a host of unnecessary policies, procedures, forms and bottlenecks at local, state and central government levels to obtain permissions and establish facilities. However, many state governments have their industry promotion departments to facilitate and support local new ventures. Raising capital for a new project is a bit difficult and time consuming because of the lack of familiarity with venture capital.

Yet, there are lots of possibilities: You can either move there and start a business, or enter into a partnership wherein you provide technology and management from the United States. The latter model has been very successful for a lot of people, especially because of the Internet. You can also bring about new business practices and joint venture partnerships based on the successes of your American business experience.

The ideal situation for NRIs is not to lose their connections with America – not to uproot everything. It may take its toll on family, but today you can be a part of both worlds in ways that were not possible some years ago. But keep in mind that three years is the minimum time frame for any new business venture in India to succeed. So if you are not prepared to wait that long, you should not do it.

It is important to look beyond these professional and business goals and focus on the possibility for NRIs to make a larger impact. Hence, the following four recommendations.

Join a Voluntary Agency

This requires a great deal of sacrifice. It is for people who have made a little bit of money, and are able to travel at their own expense. Voluntary activities going on in India need support from outside. Innovators like Bunker Roy are providing solar powered lanterns and fixing water problems in areas ranging from Rajasthan to Ladakh. His organization in Tilonia, and many others like it, need the right types of connections in terms of new technology and new volunteers with engineering backgrounds. There are many people who have gone back after gaining education and work experience in the U.S. and have been working for years in areas such as literacy, health, education, training, water, sanitation and the environment.

Content Development

One needs to have a different kind of mindset in order to do full-time voluntary work. Not everyone possesses this – and not everyone needs to. A slightly passive, yet crucial level of action can support these activities. Using the power of the Internet, people in America can begin to create the right kind of content and provide the tools for training and implementation for voluntary organizations and the public at large. That is a tremendous contribution that NRIs can make. For example, a solar power engineer who practices or teaches in the United States can create a good content package in local Indian languages about the salient features of solar power, how communities can benefit from it and how it can be implemented. This kind of work, although not glamorous, is very critical, and can be done from America and distributed to people via the Internet.

I think the Internet offers tremendous potential for NRIs to make a contribution without really leaving their workplace. This will have a significant long-term impact because the question is no longer if the Internet will reach the larger Indian population, but rather, when it will. The possibilities in these directions are endless, and I do not think they are being explored properly. Housing, literacy, creating scientific medicine – each one of us has expertise in our own areas, and within these, a lot of relevant content can be created. Steadily we can build up a large amount of content and resources to help people back home. Not that this will solve all the problems, but it would be a significant contribution.

Let's take the critical example of literacy. People can take their mother tongue, Malayalam or Oriya or whatever, and prepare programs on how to teach these languages from scratch. The need is to be creative and innovative and then have the capability to put it on the Internet, free of cost. Governments are not capable of doing these things. They will create committees and approve budgets and invite tenders, but still it wouldn't get done. All you need is someone who knows a regional language and is passionate about the cause, to spend six months or a year of free time to create a marvelous and effective program. This will be truly a significant contribution. And there are almost an infinite number of such projects that need to be completed.

Join Politics

Through politics one can bring substantial change. But in India this is very difficult and tricky, to say the least. Several people have attempted to go back and join local and national politics. Most of them have been totally frustrated because it is very difficult just to enter the political system and may take at least a decade to get established. It has become a club, and unfortunately politicians have not encouraged outside "intervention."

Become Local Heroes

We don't have local heroes in India. If you ask people to name their heroes, they will invariably name national figures – Gandhiji, Nehru, a cricketer or a film star. These Indian heroes have little to do with the realities of present day local life in India. We need to create local heroes. And that will happen when people who have emerged from their villages or towns to achieve success and prosperity return to tell their stories. This is an especially effective contribution from people who have retired from their careers.

A lot of us gained a lot from our educational institutions in India and United States I don't think we are paying our dues to our educational institutions. Its sad that after making millions, these guys don't look back and say, 'I am where I am because of IIT, or any other school I went to. Let me look at what's happening in this school or university. Is there some way I can improve it?' None of them are on educational boards. They are on corporate boards for sure. I think its time to look back at why we are where we are. And the only reason why we are where we are is because of education. If we don't participate in shaping the future of education, its not going to be what it was.

But all these things will work only when people are willing to give. Most people only want to take. People come around saying, "I want to contribute, I want to do this or that." And then they also say, "Who will pay for my ticket? Is this a job? Will I get compensation for it?" These are the people who are willing to talk, but are not willing to put any energy into their commitment. I find that 90 percent of the people who want to do something really want to do it for themselves and not for the masses. For the remaining 10 percent, all I can say is, there is a lot of work to do.

Meaningful Bottom Line

I understand that Indian business people in America, like everywhere else, have to make money. But in the process they have to link up with India - bring investments and expertise. They know that, one, the talent in India is very good, comparatively inexpensive, hardworking, sincere - and they can make money from it. Two, India is a potential market for their products and services. Three, there are frustrations in India - bureaucracy, bottlenecks, procedures, hassles - but that's given - that's part of life.

I am not one of those who say to professional Indians abroad - come back. The message I have is to be sensitive to your roots. To bridge the distance, you don't have to physically come back. You have to come back emotionally. There are a lot of things you can do while being there. You can have a virtual presence and be a virtual resource. You need to continue doing whatever you are doing, but spend some time and energy to focus on social needs here. Whether it has to do with improving education software, or giving a talk to a bunch of school kids next time you come to India - create dreams for a lot of younger people here so that they can look up and say that when I grow up I want to be like that fellow from Silicon Valley because he is from my village. So, don't cut yourselves off. Don't isolate yourself, saying I have forgotten India or I have nothing to do with India. Keep the continuity - its important.

■

FROM WORDS TO ACTIO

*India comprises a myriad of diverse cultures, faiths, beliefs and history. The cumulative effe
of this is a country rife with problems. Here is my attempt - a 10-point program - to help solv
some of them.*

Having discussed my myriad impressions of India, its people around the world, what works with them and what doesn't, at this point in this first part of the book, I would like to present a ten-point program that I feel needs to be implemented. Who am I to come up with this? I don't know – I just feel like doing it. This is a list of items that are integral for India's development and future. These are *our* needs –

1. National agenda

2. Massive political reforms

3. Decentralized decision-making

4. Population control

5. Fulfillment of basic human needs

6. Further economic liberalization

7. Infrastructure

8. Institution building

9. Human resource development

10. Change of mind-set

In the next ten chapters, including this one, I will delve into each of these points, starting with the need for India to have a National Agenda.

National Agenda

India is a country of almost one billion people without a national agenda. Everyone, every party, every group has its own agenda – but there is no national agenda. If you ask 20 people what India should be, you get 40 different answers. India as a nation must decide what we want to do, where we want to go, and when we want to go there.

Have we decided that we want to be a global economic power in the next 50 years? Have we decided that the population explosion will continue, and we will be a country of 2.5 billion people? Have we decided our strategy to be a technologically advanced country? Have we decided that we cannot go on with the present water and sanitation problems? All these issues need national debate.

This debate should start at the local panchayat or municipal level. From there, it could go to district, state, and finally the national level. It should of course also extend to people of Indian origin outside of India. This is the only way it will be the *people's* agenda. Otherwise, it will become Delhi's agenda! We cannot say that three people from each of five political parties can make a national agenda. Typically, a conference takes place in Delhi, and they decide what the national agenda is. People from every part of the country should participate and feel that they have contributed to this debate. It may take two or three years. That should not be a problem. But then we should come out with a national agenda that is more acceptable to the public.

This process requires a whole new way of thinking on communication. It would take place on TV, radio and the Internet – a national committee should be set up to coordinate these programs.

There should be a debate on a given topic for some period of time. For example, imagine the whole country discussing population, intensely for three months. All over the media, people are talking about population. This intensity in discussions will not only bring new ideas and solutions to our problems, but also perhaps more importantly, bring about consciousness and participation of a large mass of people on these topics. Seminars, meetings, programs, write-ups, articles – all happening at the panchayat level, right up to Delhi, can make a profound change. Consolidation of the inputs should take place at the state level, and then presented at the national level.

This debate will be an attempt to use democracy properly. Out of this debate would come a position paper on what we want India to be. Not that it will be acceptable to everybody or be all that accurate. But a system for debate and dialogue would then be set up, based on the use of technology. Once we get people talking, actions start to happen.

■

2 : POLITICAL REFORM

Political reform in India has to begin with an infusion of new blood. We need doctors, engineers, scientists, businessmen and people with visionary qualities to enter politics to revamp our political system through innovative ideas. That is one way the public's faith in the political system may be restored.

We have entered the 21st century, and this is going to be very different from what we have experienced in the past, especially in the time since independence. The people in the information business recognize that we are now in the Information Age. And this really means that a whole set of processes in business and government is going to change. People are already talking about electronic government and reforms of the nature that we have never seen before. Unless we get people in the government and in politics in general with that kind of a vision for the future, I think we will always remain where we are.

Lack of Visionaries

One of the problems that we have today is that we have very few visionaries in the political system. And we do not need one or two or even three. We need a minimum critical mass, a large number of people in the political system who have a professional background, and who are not in politics as a profession. Today in India, politics has become a profession, and professionals are not in politics. We need to distinguish between these two categories.

The key issue in political reform is to bring in more professionals. And by professionals I do not necessarily imply lawyers; there are a lot of lawyers in politics. By professionals I mean engineers, doctors, scientists, businessmen, and others. So unless we get the right kinds of people in the mainstream, we are not going to see reforms.

Outdated Parliamentary Form of Government

India has outlived the utility of the existing Parliamentary system. In our system today, it appears that we will always be getting minority, coalition governments. Nobody is really going to emerge with a significant majority. As a result, whosoever is in power is going to spend more time and energy trying to remain in power. What we need, and I am not necessarily advocating a Presidential system, is a system where one who comes into a position of power is given a period of stability and security, so that they do not wind up spending too much time and energy in trying to consolidate their position to be in power.

Perhaps we can have a presidential system of government, different from the American system in the sense that the President would not be elected directly. There would be an indirect election of the Prime Minister. Once elected, he remains there — not as a coalition party candidate, but as a national candidate.

Election Reforms

The third issue is election reforms. Mr. T. N. Seshan (former Chief Election Commissioner) and others have tried to do their bit, and I think they have done a reasonably good job. But it needs to be carried forward – and further. But this is at the top level.

At the bottom level, the whole system of Panchayat Raj that we are trying to put into place is not really equipped to deal with the local issues. For one, people are not trained to run local government. Just by setting up a local government, you cannot guarantee that you have capable people to run that government.

What is happening today is that the Central Government in Delhi decides how much money each state receives – and those formulae were devised many years ago, and do not make sense anymore. India has very poor local tax collection capabilities. One of the things that impressed me about the U.S. when I came here in the sixties was local tax collection. The local government is active; the tax you pay is used for developing schools, building roads, and so on. That is the essence of democracy. It can reach out over the entire country if there is a financial system in place to spend at the local level.

Break up Bigger States

I do not think we can manage a nation with only 20-25 major states. We need to break up into smaller, more manageable states. Why can't India have 50 states? What is so sacred about 20-25 states? Punjab is a good sized state – UP, Bihar, Madhya Pradesh, Maharashtra, they are all too big. Today, the national budget, state budget, and everything else, is done in Delhi. Once we have smaller states, we would be able to decentralize the government and decision making.

In conclusion, I would say that political reforms would tie up all these issues – from the top level to the bottom. The public has lost respect for politicians. People say that corruption is a major issue in politics today – maybe it is, maybe it is not. But in public perception, it is. This perception has to change and people have to feel that the leaders are there to serve them – an idea that has disappeared over the decades.

■

*Hierarchy is a pervasive phenomenon in India that exists from society to governmen
Decisions are made top down. What is required, on the contrary, is a decentralized form of go
ernment that pushes decision-making as far down as possible - to the local level.*

I find that because of our past, the Indian mindset, even today, is feudal and hierarchical. It starts right from the family, where the father, considered to be the head of the family, is supposed to have all the answers. But each member of the family should be able to think for him or herself, and for the family as a whole. But because of our hierarchical thinking, we always tend to centralize decision-making with the father.

On the other extreme of the spectrum of human society is the government. In India, all decisions are made at the central level in Delhi. As a result, the states, districts and blocks have very little autonomy. The tax collection system is also structured in a similar way – the center collects all the money. And as the saying goes, the one who has the gold, tends to make the rules. In this case, it is the center that has the gold, and so the center makes the rules too! Then, based on some old formula that was devised almost 50 years ago, the center delivers money to the states for their development.

What India really needs is to push decision-making as far down in the system as possible – to the Panchayat level. The local government should make decisions on local issues. But even this is of no value if a decentralized tax collection scheme does not exist. As a result of today's system, people feel frustrated because they feel that they have no control over their destiny. What good is making decisions at the Panchayat level, when they have to get their money from the state or national capital?

The Indian educational system is another glaring example of the flawed centralized approach. Examinations in most educational institutions in India are conducted at the end of the year. There is no semester system with exams taking place every few weeks or months. There is a board exam in high schools and entrance exams for universities and institutes. Everything in the educational system is too centralized. The a direct result of this is the lack of commitment from students and teachers toward serious education.

Training to Handle Power

Today, I do not think the machinery is set up to inform people of the knowledge that is necessary to make decisions in a decentralized system. Though we have the Panchayat in place now, there is very little training that informs the people in the Panchayat of what they are supposed to do and how to do it. In a village there may be a Panchayat of ten people, but there may not be one among them who has the basic knowledge of how to manage money and finances effectively.

People in India feel they have no power. They are constantly waiting for somebody else to make decisions. The village is waiting for the district, the district is waiting for the state and the state is waiting for the center. Thus, decentralizing decision-making and offering individuals the training to facilitate it, is a way to empower people.

Public Participation

In the Indian tax system, income tax is a very small part of total revenue collection. A very small percentage of the billion people in India pay tax. So you have very few people paying large amounts in tax, as opposed to having lots of people paying small amounts in tax. In the U.S., if you even make $20,000 per year, you have to pay some tax – even if it is only $50. In India, the minimum income above which an individual has to pay tax has been increasing. So today if you make Rs. 30,000, you do not pay any tax. I would rather have a system where someone making even Rs. 10,000 would have to pay tax, even if it was only Rs. 50. Somewhere in their hearts, people want to be honest. They want to feel that they are contributing to the financial well being of the country.

Decentralization at the Corporate Level

In India, families run a large percentage of companies, especially the small to medium sized ones. They are often not run professionally, with only the family members making decisions and other professionals simply following the instructions given.

In the public sector, key high-level bureaucrats make decisions. If you go to the offices of some of the public sector institutions, the managing director's office is very big and clean. But as soon as you walk out, the rest is a disaster. When I became Chairman of the Telecom Commission, on the very first day, someone came to give me a key to my bathroom. So, the Chairman of the Telecom Commission has his own bathroom! That's ridiculous! These are clearly the reflections of a hierarchical system. And I think that this is a fundamental national problem. As a result, a lot of human resources are wasted because people feel that they are not being allowed to do their jobs. They do not feel empowered. And that is where the connection between the decentralization of decision-making and the empowerment of people lies.

Too Much!

When I was in charge of technology missions in India, we found that there were 320 different forms for immunizations all over the country. In this case, we had the problem of too much decentralization where everybody does their own thing and there are no standards. That is not the decentralization I am talking about. We need decentralization that is governed by standards. Unfortunately, in India decentralization has often been seen as, "Let me do my own thing."

Thus on the one hand we have to centralize to establish standards, while on the other hand; we have to decentralize decision-making and implementation.

Using Technology Toward Decentralization

Technology can play a very important role in the process of decentralization. Information technology in particular, brings about openness, accessibility, connectivity, networking, democratization and decentralization. As a result, it brings about social transformation. Thus information technology is the key to decentralization. Information should be distributed freely to everyone. It is information that will empower people.

In India, the common element running through all processes is centralization. As a result of this, all data is centralized. There is very little data available to the people. We tried to break that cycle in the late 1980's by computerizing government records, such as land records, so everyone could access them. But people in power do not like that because they lose authority. Information is power. People do not like to share power. And decentralization is all about sharing power.

Decentralization of information has to be done at various levels. For school admissions, for instance, I should be able to get on a computer terminal and fill out a form. The days of walking down to the school, filling out hard copies of the form, in triplicate, and submitting it physically, should be over.

The systems are not open in India. As a result, there is a lot of manipulation. When trying to install a materials management system in any company in India, one will face heavy resistance from the people in the purchasing department, because the system will prevent them from giving contracts to their in-laws and cousins. With an open system, everybody can find out who got the contract. This kind of opening up, at all levels across the board and across the country, will bring about social transformation. Decentralization automatically makes systems open because it means a lot more people are involved. Additionally, with open systems, there will be less corruption.

The License Raj in the India of yester-years said, "You come to me if you have to produce anything. I will decide how much you can produce and when you can produce it." In the past few years, that notion has been systematically dismantled. Still, the underlying mindset is based on controls. These controls have to go, procedures have to be simplified, and new processes have to be set in place.

For instance, how do you open a bank account in India? Today, you need an introduction from two people who have an account in the same bank. Now that's a centralized procedure. The logic is that some people may be laundering money. Well, then let some people launder money – but don't harass 99 percent of the people because of the remaining 1 percent. The logic has always been that maybe someone is doing something wrong so we need to improve the procedure. It should be the other way round: improve the procedure so that we may catch someone doing something wrong. And yet, despite these procedures, rules and regulations, people are doing unlawful things all around.

A systematic examination of the problems and inefficiencies in systems, procedures, rules and regulations in India will trace them back to centralized control. That has to change. Let people do things that need to be done.

∎

4 : POPULATION IMPLOSION

Containing the ever-burgeoning population in India is an uphill and challenging task, but a crucial one, nonetheless. A large population puts pressure on limited resources and unless we teach the virtues of a small family to adults as well as children, India's progress in the new millennium will be severely hampered.

India has reached a major milestone that was flashed all over the world: the nation's population reached the one billion mark. At this rate, India will overtake China in the near future. It is hard to imagine that 50 years ago, at the time of Independence, India's population was only about 300 million. Currently, about 300 million to 400 million people in India live below the poverty line, residing in shanties and slums everywhere. To me, this is the key issue going forward in the twenty-first century.

All over the Western world, the population is aging and decreasing. In India, it is predominantly young and growing, a trend that has significant implications. When it comes to population studies, there are two schools of thought in India. One says: Don't worry about the population; we have enough resources. Look at agriculture - at one time we thought we couldn't feed 500 million. Now we can feed a billion.

The second argument goes something like this: Irrespective of whether we can supply the food or not, the pressures of increasing population on resources is unbearable. Water, land, sanitation, environment and other important resources are being impacted. Our cities are overcrowded, sanitation is a major concern nationwide, water tables are going down further and there is no way we can manage to supply the growing demand in some states.

As an example, consider the environment. Forests in India, which used to comprise 33 percent of the country's land, have been cut down to nine or 10 percent. We must now take note of these changes, understand the implications of these changes and do something drastic to reverse the trend. How are we going to cope with the need to create so many schools, colleges and jobs? Even if we create 20 million jobs a year, we cannot meet the aspirations of our youth.

Beyond Government Programs

For the past at least 30 or 35 years, we have been talking about population control and management, even introducing programs. But somehow these programs have had little impact on the numbers, as is now obvious.

In the past, we have relied on government alone for population control. I remember seeing the government's slogans like *"Ham do, hamare do,"* adorning the backs of buses. I don't think those programs have had any impact. Unfortunately Sanjay Gandhi's emphasis on population control backfired. The media reported stories of young men being forced to undergo surgery in order to meet quotas in some areas. This campaign became more like a reign of terror and put the population control program in India almost 10 years behind.

Female Literacy & Infant Mortality

I have maintained, especially when I worked with the Technology Mission created by the Rajiv Gandhi government, that population growth was dependent on two issues: women's literacy and infant mortality. A mother who is literate — who knows how to read, write and sign her name, and understands what's on government forms — is an enlightened mother in a rural setting. When only the father is literate, it does not guarantee that the family will be literate.

Wherever we managed female literacy and infant mortality, we have controlled population growth. Kerala is a classic example. This state has one of the best records in human services. It's a matriarchal society, female literacy is high and infant mortality is as low as that of some European countries. As a result, women in Kerala are having two children on the average, which means that the population of Kerala may actually be going down. Northern states, especially Uttar Pradesh and Bihar, which are backward in both women's literacy and infant mortality, both have high rates of population growth.

The past years provide one clear lesson: Government programs will not work. Unless institutions, organizations and individuals come up with separate agendas of their own, we will never be able to control the rate of growth of population. Rather than relying on government programs, communities will have to take on this task by initiating measure to improve female literacy, lower infant mortality and also create a network for sharing information on population management.

Thailand Did It Well

One man, Mechai Viravaidya, who was trained in Australia as an economist, was the driving force behind a grassroots population-control program in Thailand that is internationally considered one of the most successful. Viravaidya's mother was Scottish and his father was Thai, and they were both dedicated physicians. When he returned home in the mid-1960s after his studies, his mother told him, "You got an education not because you are bright, but because we had the money. If people like you work for profit, who is going to work for the poor?"

After a string of positions in the government, Viravaidya founded the Population and Community Development Association, a nonprofit group that spread the message of birth control in the hinterlands. He openly discussed all kinds of population issues on national television and through other media, introducing several innovative, humorous campaigns. Today, Thailand's population growth remains at its 1991 level of slightly over 1 percent and is a model for other developing countries. Mechai's name is said to be so synonymous with prophylactics in Thailand that when people ask for a "mechai," it means they want a condom! In recognition of these achievements, he was given the Ramon Magsaysay Award.

Although India's temples are full of sculptures portraying sexual themes, sex education is still taboo. We still have problems showing people kissing in movies. The resistance to sex education has restricted the ability of young people to understand birth-control techniques. This is hypocrisy.

Children Will Bring Change

When I came here to America in 1964, smoking was very acceptable and fashionable. Over a period of time, the anti-tobacco lobby slowly worked, right up from the schools. The children of parents who smoked forced them to give it up. So the children became sort of campaigners for the anti-smoking movement. Look at the implications: It has slowly built up to the situation today where smoking is banned in almost all public places in the U.S. In California, recently, smoking was banned even in bars and clubs!

You have to go after population with that kind of zeal. Schoolchildren in India have to be told about the virtues of a small family. Each family will have to recognize that it is a part of a larger community. If they have fewer children, those children will get better opportunities. But these parents will have to be told that first, if they have two children, they will survive; and second, that in the social system, to have a boy or a girl doesn't matter – they are your children and they will take care of you. India doesn't have Social Security as the U.S. does, so people consider their children to be their social security. The people have to be shown that there are other means of security – retirement benefits, pension plans, etc. We have to devise a mechanism similar to Social Security. Then people will know they will be taken care of when they are old.

Solving Problems at Home

Whenever I look at successful Indians in Silicon Valley and elsewhere, I am proud of their success and proud of being Indian. But I also feel that we have spent a lot of time solving the problems of the West, but spent so little time in solving the problems of India. If some of these people don't return to India and help solve the nation's vital problems, the population burden will become so heavy that we will have an even larger divide between the haves and have-nots. Free-market economy, globalization and privatization are helping the creation of wealth, but it is not solving larger social problems. I don't see a trickle-down effect of wealth.

I am glad that world attention on India passing the billion mark will have prompted us to begin to focus on creating new ways and means to lower population to a level at which it will not create undue pressures on limited resources. I hope the billion mark turns out to be a peak, and not just a point in a growth curve. To me, the ideal population in India would be about 600 or 700 million. How do we arrive at this figure?

There cannot be a five-year agenda for population control. It can't be for the next election! The target should be long term: that by the year 2050, India's population must be back to 700 million. Chalk out a complete plan in the next two years and go for it in the next 50.

Let us project that all women in India of childbearing age should be literate, and the infant mortality rate, which is presently about 76 per 1000, should be brought down to 25 per 1000. If we take these two objectives and have a proper communication and implementation strategy, I think we can first bring the population growth down to zero, and then take it below zero so that the population starts to decrease at the rate at which it is growing now. Then think what India can do in 50 years! If the economic growth continues at 7 to 8 percent, and the population is down to 700 million – what an impact it will have! India may then be the most powerful nation in the world.

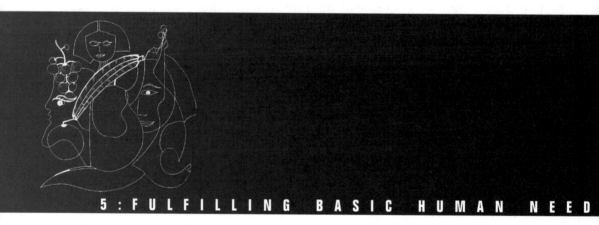

5: FULFILLING BASIC HUMAN NEED

Roughly 300 million people in India live below the poverty line. For them, the basic huma
needs of water, sanitation, food, shelter, clothing and education remain largely unfulfilled. Th
government cannot achieve this alone; the community needs to get involved.

What do basic human needs imply in a country like India? As I see it, 'basic human needs' means water, sanitation, food, clothing, shelter and literacy. I think India has a long way to go in fulfilling these basic human needs for a large majority of its people. There are about 300 million people in India who are below the poverty line. And compared to the rest of the world, India's poverty line is very low. Unless we lift these 300 million people above this low 'Indian' poverty line and give them respectable living standards, development will have no meaning. The prosperity of a few at the top does not mean much unless the average comes up substantially. Every society should always be judged by how well the poorest of its poor are doing.

The problem of basic human needs that India faces today has not always existed. Earlier, India had far fewer people, and thus, less strain on its natural resources. Industrialization has led to environmental degradation, further aggravating the problem. The nature of the problem has thus changed over the decades as well. The issues concerning each of these needs are very different from what they were 50 years ago. The area of basic human needs is a highly complex one today, where there are connections and interconnections that need to be taken into consideration while planning.

Water & Sanitation

In hundreds of thousands of villages in India, there is no proper drinking water – water that is potable, free of excess iron and other chemicals, and easily accessible. When women in India no longer have to walk over a mile to get drinking water, then we can consider that the issue of water in India has been addressed.

On any train journey, look around in the morning and you will see hundreds of people squatting all over. It's pathetic. It's a disgrace for a country like India, that in the 21st century, there are no basic sanitation facilities for millions. We can send satellites into space, but we cannot solve sanitation problems!

There are a lot of voluntary agencies, like Sulabh Shauchalya, that are doing excellent work to address this problem. But sanitation is a very critical issue – it is linked with water and health, and it has not been addressed properly.

But again, it isn't entirely the government's task to address the issue of sanitation. It is the people who have to get into it. People have to realize that this is in the community's interest, and that proper sanitation facilities for everybody in the community is important for their health.

Who Can Do It?

Basic human needs cannot be fulfilled by the government alone. In India, the government has given an impression to the people that it will take care of their basic needs. It hasn't done it because it can't do it and isn't equipped to do it. People haven't learnt this lesson after 50 years of independence. These are community issues and should be addressed by the people.

People in India are ready to complain about their problems all the time! Go to any village in India and they will tell you that the schoolteacher has run away, the water pump hasn't been working for the last six months, the *gobar* gas plant doesn't work, and so on. What they really mean is that the government in New Delhi should come and solve their problems — because that's the impression that the government itself has given them! Instead, the message should be that these are not problems that the government can solve; they are best left in the hands of the community. The problem-solving attitude has to come from the people – 'I must learn how to fix the water-pump,' or 'I must make sure that the teacher in the village school is happy, so that he continues to teach my children,' and so on.

This community feeling — that these are my problems and I have to solve them — has not been cultivated. As a result, people always look to somebody else to solve their problems and never take the initiative themselves. Thereby, the areas of the basic needs remain neglected.

Shelter

We made an attempt during the '80s to evolve a process where we could create 10 million jobs in India every year. In that process, we analyzed how much it would cost to create one new job in various industries. That is, for a given amount of investment, which industry creates the maximum number of jobs? To my surprise, we learned that it is the construction industry, which requires the lowest amount of investment to create one new job – as a mason, bricklayer, plumber and electrician. The cost of creating a job in telecom, for instance, was about Rs. 125,000, whereas just about Rs. 10,000 to 20,000 could create one new job in construction.

When you look at the slums in the major cities in India and the housing conditions in the villages, the situation is miserable. All the main raw materials for basic construction come from the earth – wood, mud, brick and so on, and it creates a great number of jobs!

Unfortunately, the types of institutions that can fuel the growth of construction don't exist in India. Unlike in other parts of the world, there are no mortgage institutions that can give people loans for buying or building a house that can be paid back over 30 years. On the other hand, there are a lot of housing schemes, but they are insignificant compared to what India needs as a whole. Thus it is a Catch-22 situation. A part of the solution lies in standardization.

Standards

I believe that the key to efficient housing and construction in India is standards. There are no standards in India – no standard doors, windows, nails, bricks, and so on. In the Western world, everything in construction is standard. But the situation in India is exemplified by the fact that the Bureau of Standards comes under the Department of Civil Supplies and not under the Ministry of Industry, as it should. Can you imagine that there is no standard brick in India – anyone can make whatever kind of brick he wants! If all these things are standardized, there will be production equipment of the same type, there will be factories for mass production of bricks, and the entire construction industry will be streamlined. Wherever there are standards, many people participate, the volumes increase and the costs go down. That's the whole purpose of standards all over the world.

There could even be standardized jhopar-pattis (slum-dwellings), so that people can go and buy one for Rs. 500 or so and boom! — it can be put together as a place to live. Since this does not exist, people beg, borrow and steal tires, plastic bags, sheets, bamboo sticks, tin cans and jute to construct a *jhopar-patti*. The result: messy and inconsistent slums all over urban India.

Main Issues

For decades, the issue of basic human needs, for some reason or another, has not been given the priority it deserves. There has been mere lip service, just as in the case of population control. There is a need to put together real task forces for all these issues, set a time-bound program, and get the job done! We haven't put in the energy that is required to make these things happen.

The important issues for addressing basic human needs are communication, education, technology and the involvement of people through voluntary agencies. This would empower them, so that they in turn realize that it is their problem and not the government's. Finally, we need modern management methods, such as an implementation program and monitoring controls to ensure that the agendas are addressed and that people deliver what they promise.

Romance of Problem Solving

Those years that I spent in India, trying to understand and solve the country's massive problems were, in a sense, romantic. It was like being on a high all the time. But everybody else just couldn't see eye to eye with us. We were living in a problem-solving world, but many of those around us were living in a problem-identification world.

The main goal should be to see how technology can help expedite the process of fulfilling basic human needs and enhance the process of modernization. Technology can only be an entry point and not an end point. By being an entry point, it could bring substantial changes, including changes in the mindset of the people. Technology becomes critical in reducing cost, improving productivity and efficiency, and organizing systems so that some standards are established. And these are monumental problems that cannot be solved by five or 10 people. It requires a massive team effort. If things have not worked in the past, then what should we do next? We have to constantly think of new ways of solving the same problems. That is the main challenge.

■

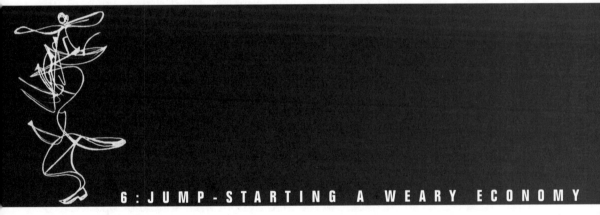

6: JUMP-STARTING A WEARY ECONOMY

The real impetus of economic liberalization was spearheaded in Rajiv Gandhi's era. Since then, a lot has been achieved in terms of higher foreign exchange reserves and higher inflow of foreign investments. Nevertheless, there are miles to go before we sleep.

Though India actively started to liberalize its economy in the early part of the 1990s, the real impetus for liberalization started in the 1980s — in Rajiv Gandhi's era. During that time, India's balance sheet looked fairly good and the exchange rate was about Rs. 10 to a dollar. By the time people began discussing reforms, the rate was Rs. 16 to 17, ultimately dipping to the Rs. 45 - 50 range today.

Ideas leading to economic liberalization were being discussed in public forums. Corporatization of government departments, improving productivity and efficiency, reducing cost, selling parts of public-sector companies to private investors, creating a better stock market — all these things were being discussed, even to the point of removing foreign exchange controls. It was hoped that liberalization would take root quickly and many Indian companies would be privatized.

However, none of these ideas found political support for real implementation. Parliament never took this debate to a conclusion and the administration felt equally uncomfortable implementing these ideas. As a result, we had to wait until 1991, when the country's balance sheet looked so bad, that we needed the support of the World Bank and the International Monetary Fund (IMF). They, in turn, agreed to help only if structural reforms were made in the economy. Thus political support for liberalization came under bad circumstances, when there was almost no other option available.

The Narasimha Rao government in 1991 began something that should have really been done in the '70s. Today, we can see the benefits of liberalization on a macro level: Foreign exchange reserves have improved substantially and a fair amount of foreign investment has come in. Nevertheless, a lot still needs to be done.

Potato Chips vs. Microchips

There has been an active debate in the media about what should be opened to private enterprise. It's a debate between "potato chips" and "microchips." The investor's perspective is very different from the administration's.

If India doesn't manufacture and distribute everything efficiently, there will be foreign competition that will come in and do so. I have always believed that you need to build internal competition first, before building external competition. Unfortunately, internal competition does not occur unless there is a threat from the outside. India is a huge market and companies around the world are interested in doing business there. For real economic reform, the systems have to be transparent and open, and the policies have to be kept stable for a significant period of time. There has to be clarity for at least three to five years for investors, in terms of tax structures and all the other resources required to do business. Only then will substantial changes be seen.

In addition, there is the issue of whether India is capable of creating its own multinationals. There are a lot of companies within India, which can produce quality goods and services, and their performance is directly related to competition and economic liberalization.

Ongoing Liberalization

A revolutionary new plan cannot be executed in isolation. An ecology always needs to be developed before appropriate results can be attained. First, and perhaps most importantly, India has failed to understand, appreciate and develop an ecology of privatization and liberalization. This means that we have tried to implement liberalization in isolation, without properly understanding the implications and inter-relationships among its various aspects. The most important thing to remember is the regulatory framework.

Further, in India, market forces don't really get free play because there are artificial barriers. In addition, black money is still a very large part of the equation of the overall economy. A very small percentage of people in India pay tax. As a result, the government's revenue predominantly comes from indirect taxes — central excise tax, custom duties, and so on. These, in turn, bog down the economy. Thus, economic liberalization is also linked with the need for a new kind of tax structure.

Another aspect that plays a very important role in the economic liberalization is labor law. You can't really hire and fire people in India. And that makes it very difficult to compete effectively in the global market because there is always excess baggage to carry around.

The key to a successful next phase of economic liberalization is an integrated policy that incorporates all these elements. Underlying these three are administrative reforms targeted at efficient implementation.

Implementation Issues

The Indian mindset is monopolistic. It is oriented toward a public sector presence. As a result, it is difficult to ask a vested interest group to liberalize its own sector. For example, the Department of Telecom is asked to liberalize telecom. Consequently, they see competition coming in and threatening them. At the same time they find themselves in a situation in which they have to open up. They don't like to do that, because their own jobs are at stake.

Thus, everybody else doesn't get a fair play, because the department is setting the rules of the game. New players demand fair treatment with respect to tariff structure, revenue sharing, interconnection agreements, and so on. All of this requires the monopoly to be responsive, and they've not been responsive enough in encouraging privatization yet.

India has hardly ever used any major external consultancy on a large scale for implementation. So, on the one hand the regulatory authority sets the rules of the game. On the other hand, the same bureaucrats and administrators try to get liberalization on track! Help should be sought from a few top consultants to get global expertise in setting up various frameworks and systems.

Furthermore, there's never been a broad national timetable on the liberalization of each sector. It's taking its sweet time. There's never been an independent body looking at the implementation. It's been part of a government process, rather than part of a national agenda.

Media Management

India has failed to manage the media to create a climate of cooperation for the short and long term benefits of liberalization. The country didn't systematically organize the media to mold public opinion and stimulate public pressure so that all the stakeholders could come together and look at issues that affect consumers. This includes educating members of Parliament, legislative assemblies, workers at the federal and the state level, bureaucracy and the administration. They have to be advised to the effect: "Your job before liberalization was like this, but after liberalization it's going to be like this." This is a massive task. It cannot be done at an individual level. It can only be done after creating the proper climate, and then offering education. This process is also part of the ecology, but is somewhat separate because in a democracy, if properly handled, this could create a fair amount of pressure to expedite the entire process.

Labor leaders have not been properly educated about the benefits of liberalization. They hear bits and pieces, and then they simply discuss the issues among themselves. All those discussions focus on what the situation is today, and how liberalization will disturb the balance, as opposed to how far-reaching the benefits will be and how labor can capitalize on this process. Because of this, labor leaders who have a Marxist, public sector mindset see liberalization as a threat. They fear a loss of security and pension benefits. They only think about what they will lose, rather than what they will gain.

Telecom labor leaders in India often call me to discuss new major policy developments. In discussing the issues, they are receptive and open, but don't really get the full picture. Even while talking to me, they are sort of talking to themselves. Immediately after they hang up, they consult each other, rather than reach out to people who are for liberalization and try to understand the other point of view. Overall, the situation has always been "us vs. them." But the attitude has to be: "We are all part of liberalization. Let's see how we will move forward."

Pizza vs. Clean Water

It is important to analyze the impact of the liberalization that has already been accomplished. At the national level, one visible impact is the improvement in the foreign exchange situation. This has reduced the pressure from international funding agencies.

Secondly, liberalization has affected the urban population more than the rural population of India. In urban areas, now you can freely get better products and services — automobiles, food, clothing and almost everything else — things that were not really available before. But very few people have access to these services and can afford them.

So the real fruits of liberalization haven't reached the large number of India's rural population. They are not part of the equation yet. What is more critical to them is basic human needs. With liberalization, has the delivery of water improved? Sanitation, housing, education? Getting better pizza in India is of no concern to them.

Let's Run With It!

If you look at the past few years, entrepreneurs in India have restricted their business interests to the urban elite market — electronics, cosmetics, consumer goods, fashion, etc. But what is really needed is to take the new liberalized environment in the country and run with it! They need to explore and create new markets that will bolster the local economy of each region in the country and complement their skills. Innovation and initiative is an integral part of economic liberalization. India has made a successful start with the process of economic liberalization — but considering international developments, we still have a long way to go if the country is to become a major global player within the next decade. An integrated, strategic-thinking approach, not a bit-by-bit approach, is going to be the key to success.

Finally, China has 50 million mobile phones today, compared to 3.5 million in India. This simple statistic puts India's entire liberalization process in perspective. In other words, we have a long way to go.

■

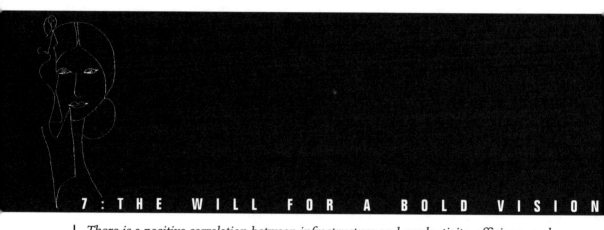

7: THE WILL FOR A BOLD VISION

There is a positive correlation between infrastructure and productivity, efficiency and prosperity. Although India's infrastructure is functioning, it is largely outdated and needs to be overhauled entirely. In this chapter, I will discuss two elements of infrastructure - power and transportation.

India has accomplished a great deal in power, transport and communication. Take for instance the Indian Railways. This network is one of the most powerful train networks in the world – very large, carrying millions of people over hundreds of thousands of miles, and fairly well-managed. Fifty years ago, there was no power in the villages; it is there now. A telephone is within reach in most of the areas of the country. So we have tried to take transport, power and communication – the key components of a country's infrastructural development – into every area of the country.

But it's still not enough. Go anywhere in India, and you will see power cuts, traffic jams, crowded trains and dead telephones – all pointing to poor infrastructure in the country. There is a direct connection between infrastructure and productivity, efficiency and prosperity. The major reasons for underachievement are inadequate policies and investment, and poor management. And whatever has been done has been hampered by population growth. We have simply not kept up with the times.

Let us here consider the first two aspects of infrastructure, i.e., power and transportation.

A Different Approach to Power

The Indian government has made some efforts toward privatization of power. There are two issues here: Allowing new private power generation utilities to come up; and converting existing power utilities to private ownership – whether on the stock market, or by putting them in the hands of professional management.

Power is a key necessity in India, but its privatization raises several issues. First, of course, there is a need for political will, which will lead to administrative reforms, financial reforms, as well as changes in tariff structure, labor laws and ecological laws. Privatization of power utilities in isolation wouldn't make sense.

But go anywhere in the country and you will notice that people just swing wires and tap into the power lines. Further, there are incredible fluctuations in the power supply. When you are supposed to get a steady 220 volts, sometimes you get 120 and sometimes 270! India probably spends more money in making power stabilizers than it would in fixing the system's deficiencies.

Thus, the power infrastructure in India needs to be not only expanded, but also cleaned up. Every state is looking for more power. Traditionally, we have always gone after large power plants. I think it's time to look at smaller and medium-sized power projects. With large power plants, besides several managerial concerns, there is also the major issue of distribution over long distances. This results in substantial waste during transmission.

In the final analysis, the whole power situation in India needs to be worked on from three angles:

1. All existing state electricity boards (state government bodies that manage the power utilities) need to be substantially modernized in management, so that their productivity and efficiency is comparable with international standards. With the existing system in India, this is a very complicated task because everyone involved is a government employee lacking in independence and autonomy. The power ministry controls all procedures and its laws were set down a long time ago. One approach is to corporatize them and thereafter take them public at the appropriate time. The other would be to privatize them.

2. Create substantially higher power capacity in the country by inviting local and foreign investment.

3. Focus on alternate energy sources, such as solar and wind energy.

Road Hazard

Any way you look at it, India's road system is a disaster. The highways are rundown, poorly constructed, unprotected, dangerous and inadequate by a long shot. There is no basic system of multiple-lane highways—something that almost every other nation has been able to construct.

Part of the reason for this is land acquisition. First, land acquisition policies are not strong. Second, land prices have soared, making acquisition very expensive. It is thus extremely difficult for private parties to succeed in building and operating highways without government support in land acquisition. If the acquisition was done 30 to 40 years ago, even though the highways were not built, we would have been better off.

All the major metropolitan and industrial cities in the country need to be connected through a national grid of multiple-lane international-standard highways. This is very expensive. But some experiments should be done with privatization of roads to gain some experience. The quality of construction has consistently gone down in India and must be brought back up. Enough digging is not done for construction of regular roads, resulting in weak roads that break easily. Government contractors bribe the officials and then use poor materials and workmanship to make an extra buck. Then the roads break and the same contractor gets the job again! The weather, especially the monsoon season, is not kind on the roads either.

India's ports also need immediate attention. Waterways have not been used as effective transport systems. Of course, the weather cycle is such that there are annual floods and annual droughts. We need to understand this situation, work around it, and use the water systems effectively. There was a plan put forth by K V Rao to link all the rivers, which was deemed very expensive then. But when you look at it today, considering all the benefits it would have brought, it looks worthwhile. I wish we had done it.

Unlikely as it may sound, there is one way that India can leapfrog its transportation problem – by creating a good air transport system using small planes, even in rural areas. This needs to be carefully evaluated: Is it possible to create a really good air transport system in India – for small airlines and small cargo planes?

Urban Transportation

Public transport in almost all Indian cities is in a hopeless condition. What we need is good underground transportation – metros. Calcutta has shown that it can be done, though it took 15 years and is limited in reach. Yet, it is well maintained, it works, people are proud of it and it has made a tremendous difference to the city. It is important to recognize this now and take the initiative in providing underground public transport in all major cities. I know it is expensive, but it's time to bite the bullet. Public transport is the key to urban development – and that's infrastructure.

How to Bite the Bullet

During the early eighties, every three or four months I used to go to Tianjing, a city near Beijing in China. Once I went after a gap of a year, and I couldn't recognize the city. Driving in, I asked if we were really in Tianjing, and the driver said that in ten months they've built 70 miles of eight-lane highway going around and into the city. They simply demolished everything and built it all up! That's the magnitude of effort needed in infrastructure. And the Chinese have done that very well. Everywhere you go, there is infrastructural construction – because they recognize that infrastructure is key for development. India has not been able to do this – not because we didn't have the investment, but because we didn't have the political will. We don't think big. We don't have a grand, national project that excites the country.

All these mega projects look expensive when you look at them on paper – but when you bite the bullet, ten years down the road they would surely look like it was the right thing to do.

I am not saying that for infrastructural development we should only do huge projects. But you need a bold vision. A vision that says, let's have eight-lane highways connecting 20 major cities in India, metro railway systems for 10 major cities, connect all the rivers with water canals, and have enough power by the year 2010. Once there is a vision like that, I think people will rally around and make it a reality.

India's New Deal

Taking inspiration from Franklin Roosevelt's New Deal, I feel that all community asset projects are national projects. Take for example the building of roads. What do you really need? Local raw materials and some capital. This capital shouldn't be looked at as carrying any risk, because with it you are building national assets and creating local jobs. But no investment will come if people feel that the government is not sound. If the system is open and international markets feel that these projects will get implemented, money will come because these projects make all other investments more secure. It will come in exactly the way it came and is coming to China, Indonesia, Malaysia and all other countries around the world that are building strong infrastructure. This is nothing new – the world has done it before.

In any case, I ask, is there any other way out? Except to delay it, and go on delaying it, as we have done till now?

■

8 : RECOGNIZE, MOBILIZE, SYNTHESIZE

Compared to international standards, Indian institutions rarely function well enough to serve the needs of the average citizen. It's time to take action to rebuild some of them because alive and strong institutions make an efficient and powerful nation.

I find that the main difference between developed and developing countries all over the world is that in developed countries, institutions are set up for average, regular human beings to function. In developing countries, however, institutions are not set up for even the most intelligent human beings to function.

Institution-building is one of the most critical tasks for nation-building. By institutions, we mean legal institutions, educational institutions, health, financial, science and technology institutions, and standards at all levels in the system. And institution building means creating and keeping institutions alive, with their main purpose and processes in tune with modern times. After independence, our founding fathers spent a lot of time and money in building institutions from scratch – the IITs are one example.

Unfortunately, a lot of these institutions are not functioning adequately, compared with international standards. Go to libraries, there are no books; in universities, there is no research; legal cases are not settled for 20 years; and so on. There has been more emphasis on bricks and mortar than form and substance. If you look around the country, you will see that institutions have land, buildings, housing, peons, paanshops and teashops, but they really don't have the kind of mindset focused on productivity and purpose.

I am not implying that all institutions are bad. There are some private institutions that are working very well – the Confederation of Indian Industry (CII), for example. Almost invariably, emphasis is given to physical infrastructure, but not human infrastructure.

Human resources in these institutions have not kept up with the modern pace. For example, why can't we use computers effectively so that all of the existing legal cases can be handled quickly, within the next few years, so that a sense of justice comes about?

Consider also the education systems, which have remained the same in the last 30 to 40 years. In a majority of schools and universities, examinations are still held once a year. Why are we not changing this into a semester system? Why are there fixed courses that do not allow students to choose what they want to study. In several places around the world there exist "study abroad programs." Similarly, in India, we should have a 'study in a different state' program. A Gujarati student can go to Kerala for a semester. This will also bring about deeper national integration. But we have no programs like this because the institutions were set up once, and the same set of rules and regulations are followed year after year.

Lack of Replication

There are many examples of remarkable success stories within India. Kerala has one of the best records on infant mortality and literacy. The city of Surat cleaned itself thoroughly after the shocking incidence of plague spreading through it. Punjab had an agricultural revolution like one perhaps not seen anywhere else in the world. But these success stories are not being replicated in other parts of the country. Has Uttar Pradesh emulated the Kerala example to increase literacy? Did Bombay or Calcutta follow Surat's example? Did Bihar try to understand how Punjab could do it? All of this is related to institution-building. Our institutions are feudal and hierarchical, with an old set of values and systems. In India, systems work on privilege and patronage instead of performance and productivity.

Developed countries reached that level because of good institutions that work. The job of the president of the United States is much easier because the institutions work. The libraries, universities, the Senate and committees really do their jobs. Everything is well set to function efficiently. You don't need anybody's help in America to get a job done because all processes to get it done are functioning. Institutions are constantly reviewed and refined. There are no other interventions to make it nonfunctional. Sadly, very little attention is paid to processes in India.

Right now there is a major information revolution sweeping the world. Among its various other benefits, information is changing the value chain. Let us look at the role of information in institution-building.

People as Infrastructure

The key to restructuring and rebuilding institutions is to change the mindset and look at new ways of doing things. For this, we don't really need to change the physical infrastructure; the focus has to be on the human infrastructure. One way is to build new institutions from scratch, so you don't carry the old baggage, like we did with the Center of Development of Telematics (C-DoT). Unfortunately, there is only a limited scope for what can be done in this manner on a national level. The majority of the work is in rebuilding the institutions. The fundamentals must be questioned – what was the purpose for which the institution was set up? Are we meeting that purpose? Is most of the budget going into salaries alone? For instance, Indian institutions have an incredible number of chaprasis (assistants) – people who do nothing but provide officers with water and tea and pass files in government offices. Is that job really necessary in this modern age? All these unnecessary activities and expenses are being incurred, and they all are counter to the spirit of building quality institutions.

How to Build Institutions

At the national level, institution-building is a very difficult and complicated task. The entire gamut of existing institutions in India must be evaluated, and in one stroke, a plan for modernization needs to be formulated. It has to be a consolidated national endeavor. It cannot and will not happen one by one. Ultimately it boils down to people. Institutions are as good as the people in them. A well-managed government is a prerequisite, where specific roles are defined and accountability exists. The government should be a structure for efficiency, planning, decentralization and reforms. Without government, you cannot expect good human resources.

Instead of progressing forward, here's what happens today in India. Let us say 10 people are put together to work out a plan for modernization of the educational system. All 10 first want a designation, a car, a house and travel to Delhi with all expenses and hotel expenses paid. However, these are peripheral activities that have nothing to do with the task at hand.

We need virtual organizations, where people do work remotely – with the highest efficiency and productivity. Many officials fly to Delhi every day to get some job done, which often only takes half an hour. A videoconferencing system can be created between every state capital and Delhi. It will be cheaper than having people fly all the time. But then, in India, a culture has been established to go travel, meet people, have tea with old chums, and then maybe discuss some work. They will not use a videoconferencing system, because they are not yet accustomed to the information culture.

First Steps

The first step is to recognize that institution-building is a major task that has not received the attention it deserves. We have to understand our institutions are dying, and urgently need to be rebuilt. I don't think we have accepted this fact in the first place. We are happy with what we've got, and we can justify it and say, "No problem, we're okay." That's the starting point for a new mindset. We've got to say, "No, we are not okay. We can't live like this. We're capable of much more!"

■

9:FOUNDATION FOR THE FUTURE

Human resource development is a vital part of nation building. The real challenge here is to open opportunities for people to develop and apply their talent, give them access to services and support that enables them to contribute to their community.

The key to nation building is human resource development. I look at this with as much passion as I have for telecom. Without focusing on people, we are not going to develop a nation. People are the heart of development, and at the same time, its architects and beneficiaries – villagers, slum dwellers, farmers, factory workers, teachers, mothers, nurses, children, students and youths – they really make things happen.

But you cannot build a nation when half of these people are illiterate. India's population has grown substantially in the last 50 years. We were hoping that by the year 2000, we could make the country 100 percent literate. In pockets, we have done very well — for example, Kerala and Gujarat — but education has not taken off as a national movement. States like Uttar Pradesh, Bihar and Madhya Pradesh have a very high illiteracy rate, especially among women. Literacy has to go beyond mere reading and writing. It must focus on raising the level of knowledge, so that all levels of society may participate. The real challenge in human resource development is to open opportunities for people to develop and apply their talent, give them access to services and support that enables them to contribute to their community. In fact, it is necessary to build and sustain an infrastructure of institutions, which encourages learning and investment in human resource development.

I worked on a special report on Human Resource Development called "Foundation for the Future" for the Commonwealth Secretariat, which was published in 1993 and presented to 50 prime ministers of Commonwealth countries. Based on the formulations presented in that report, there are five fundamental strategies that need to be focused on to develop human resources. These are:

Well-managed, Professional Government

First, there is a need to identify what a government should do and what it should not do. The basis of an effective human resource development program is a well-managed, professional government. The functions and features of this government must include a legal framework to establish and confer validity on social institutions and regulate behavior between individuals; a policy environment that promotes human resource development at all levels and in all sectors by maximizing the incentives to it and minimizing the obstacles; allocation of resources irrespective of whether the institutions are owned and managed by the government, or are in private hands; identification of what is good for the public; equity and universality – protecting and sustaining the weak and disadvantaged.

All these factors amount to a government that is goal-oriented, decentralized, and focused on quality, productivity, efficiency and accountability. But if the government is corrupt and inefficient, it sends the wrong signal to the people – i.e., "Is that what education does to government officials?"

NGOs and the Private Sector

This has not happened in India at significant levels. Private schools are not encouraged, private universities are not allowed, and giving donations to universities is very complicated. The whole education structure is so rigidly controlled by the government that it is very difficult to expand. Support from non-governmental organizations (NGOs) in human resource development is critical. One glaring inadequacy of the public sector is illiteracy among the people who work for the government and their families. Each public sector organization should make sure that it provides education to all its employees. But there is a distinct lack of sensitivity toward these issues of importance. All private sector industries should be compelled to educate all their employees. They should be allowed to hire illiterates, but part of their responsibility should be to educate them. Incentives should be given to those who will go for studies after their work hours. All this requires a commitment on the part of the government and everybody else to build a nation that is fully literate.

Priority for Women

Females constitute half of the world's population. It has been found that if the mother is literate, invariably the entire family is literate. If only the father is literate, he will probably be more interested in going out and earning, and the children's education may get ignored. So we've got to place more emphasis on female literacy. I explained in a previous chapter how female literacy and infant mortality are greatly connected with population growth. Similarly, in human resource development, the education of women is the foundation for building educated families. There is a need for gender sensitivity when tackling these issues.

Mobilization of Resources

It takes a lot of money to educate one person. But then there are a lot of creative ways to cut down that cost. For example, we found out that it takes about Rs. 600 to make one person literate. This was based on the assumption that you need classrooms, blackboards, bricks, teachers and so on. At that rate, we would not be able to make 100 million people in India literate. So we decided to turn the whole approach around and said that we could use existing government buildings as classrooms in the evenings. We could ask people to donate books and blackboards and other necessary items. This way, we could reduce the cost to Rs. 60 per person – a factor of 10.

One hundred percent literacy is a challenge; and it has to be taken as one, seriously. But that has not happened. They have talked about it in the media, but there are not enough proponents for this cause. There are exceptions, of course – several voluntary agencies in Kerala, Gujarat and other places have done a superb job. But that is not enough. These efforts must be replicated all over the rest of the country.

Use of Technology

We need technology in education and education in technology. Let me give you some simple examples which can make — and indeed, have made — a tremendous difference. To build wooden blackboards, trees have to be cut. A plastic blackboard was conceived and produced by the IPCL in Baroda, Gujarat. We found out from the Institute of Standards that there were no standards on blackboards. Three standard sizes of blackboards were created. A solar-powered lantern was developed for hilly areas so people could study after dark, without electricity or oil. So there is a lot of technology that can go into dumb, routine stuff, with tremendous results in improving the delivery system of education. But unfortunately, when we talk of technology in India, we often think only of satellites, cellular phones and computers.

The McDonald's Approach

What India has done in the past is to lay greater emphasis on higher education, at the cost of primary education. As a result, our universities have created very talented people who go abroad and work for them, leaving the nation at a loss. India's premier institutions bring out thousands of the best and brightest trained professionals, who are either picked up by foreign multinationals or go abroad.

We need to put equal, if not greater, emphasis on primary education. It is a mammoth task for a child to find a good school in any major Indian city today. There should be a McDonald's hamburger approach to primary education. The number of private schools has to increase rapidly; yet there have to be strict specified standards that they need to meet – just like McDonald's hamburgers everywhere are more or less the same.

Further, literacy has to be an ongoing activity. It's not about a one-shot deal of teaching somebody how to read and write. It's about creating an interest in learning in the individual, and making it a lifelong habit. So there is a need to set up local libraries and have special pages in local newspapers targeted to the newly literate. There are all kinds of interesting and innovative ideas that can be explored to develop better human resources.

Higher Education

I am not undermining the importance of higher education. If there are 1 billion people in the country, there are bound to be 10 million smart ones among them. We need to take those 10 million and create an institutional framework for them to work toward a better society and more jobs. So at one level we need mass education, and at the other level, we require high-quality performance for a smaller group of people, which in turn creates jobs. The country needs to capitalize heavily on the human resources it possesses.

Job Enhancement

A simple dilemma prevails throughout India: There is a high level of unemployment, with millions of graduates looking for a job. Yet, it's very difficult to get a good plumber or the right electrician or carpenter.

The reason is simple: There is a complete lack of focus on vocational education in India. The skill levels of professionals have to be expanded substantially. A carpenter probably still uses the same tools as his grandfather. He probably does not have an electric drill, power screwdriver or even a tool-bag. That's because he has not been a part of the human resource development process. Vocational education has to be tied to training in new tools – so that efficiency of work will increase; work will finish faster, bringing life and businesses into action faster; the worker will make more money; and the entire pace of the nation will speed up.

It should be made difficult to get into higher education, and easier to get into vocational education. Everybody doesn't need to get a B.A. or B.Comm. After high school, getting a two-year diploma in machine tools should be made as attractive and lucrative a proposition as a B.A.

But there is another dimension to this problem in India: Everybody wants an office job – so they don't have to do much, and yet get paid regularly!

Teaching Teachers

Teachers in India today are not equipped to fulfill the demand for greater and better education. Teachers often take pride in the fact that the notes from which they teach have not changed for 20 years. The situation should be exactly the opposite! Their notes should become obsolete every year. In teacher training, electronics can play a big role – through videos, TV or the Internet. Since teachers have already achieved a certain level of understanding, it can be refreshed and enhanced.

Human resource development is not about higher education, or computer education, or vocational education. It is about literacy and primary education. The basic goal for India should be the achievement of 100 percent literacy in the next 10 to 15 years – creating foundations for a large number of people so they can participate in a unified vision for the future.

■

10:FINALLY, IT'S ABOUT MINDSET

In India, the feudal mindset of the people has thwarted the growth of a common civil code. I am not advocating that people disregard family values, ancient customs and religious beliefs, but rather they need to change mindset, which links directly with taking action and implementing new ideas.

India's past history makes its society value a feudal and hierarchical mindset. India used to be a nation with hundreds of small princely states, whose kings called all the shots. As a nation it has been invaded by people from all over the world – the Mughals came early in this millennium, and then came the Europeans – the British, Portuguese, French and others. A handful of people representing a trading company by the name of the East India Company entered India and ended up ruling the nation for two hundred years. No one in India ever had an expansion strategy in mind. India never invaded anyone to expand its territories. Its political and social mindset was feudal, and that is why it succumbed to the smart tactics of the colonists.

India's hierarchical attitude begins with its families. The head of the household is supposed to have all the answers. The older you are, the wiser you are supposed to be. This comes from the legacy of 'oral' culture. The written culture says, "If you are young, and if you have read about some subjects, you could be an expert in that subject." The oral culture says you have to have lived long enough to assimilate all your knowledge.

This feudal and hierarchical culture creates an approach that has not evolved apparently with the times. We always talk about unity in our diversity. But we have never talked about development in diversity. That is, our developmental strategy could be based on diversity. What this means is that we must go beyond personal agenda, family agenda and community agenda to focus on a national agenda. Most of the people actually cannot go beyond a community agenda. That is why the caste system has been strong, women do not have equal rights, religious sentimentality is strong and a parochial mindset continues to prevail. In widespread areas of the country – especially states like Bihar, Uttar Pradesh, Madhya Pradesh and Rajasthan, nothing has changed for centuries. That is what constitutes the nation, not a handful of educated people. The direction and speed at which these states move, is how India itself moves.

No Common Civil Code

Due to these tendencies, we have not been able to evolve a common civil code. You cannot build a forward-moving, strong nation that does not have a unified social vision. Because of the inability to go beyond personal, family and community agendas, we do not respect public laws. Of course, we always respect personal laws – how to deal correctly with your father-in-law, what rituals to perform during marriage, or exactly how to offer prayers on a specific occasion. Some of this is not even written anywhere, but somehow people know what to do and how to do it. But when it comes to public laws – paying tax, following traffic lights and garbage disposal – people do not follow rules. This is because they do not respect the larger agenda. They do not understand building community assets. Because of this frame of mind, we have not been able to fully utilize our human capital.

Indians may be poor. India is definitely not poor. Look at its art, heritage, architecture, music, food, clothing – we have so many assets. But the thinking today is, "We are a poor nation. We cannot accomplish this, we cannot do that." What the nation collectively did, and how it behaved worked in the past. India was powerful – people came here for education, hope, wisdom and commerce. The change came with the effects of extended colonization – when we became a dependent nation. There is now the mammoth task of bringing it back to a modern, independent mode of thinking.

Having been to South Africa a few times, I can appreciate what imprint apartheid has left on the culture there. People are unable to think they are capable of competing in the world today, because they were conditioned by imperialism to think that they are inferior. And it will take a long time, even several generations to be released of that mindset.

Incremental Change Not Enough

In India there is the *Brahmanical* science and the *Sudra* science. The former says speak at seminars, go to international conferences and present papers. But do not fix a broken plug. Hey, you do not even have to know how to fix it – that is a Sudra's job. And this percolates down all the way in the Indian system. It's a very hierarchical, feudal system. Indian democracy is based on perks, privilege and patronage.

Furthermore, there has been very little focus on performance. Who you know is more important than what you want to do. If you are looking for quick results, nothing happens. You need lots and lots of patience. When people figure out that you mean well and you are not going to go away, then the doors open, and the support you get from the public is tremendous. All kinds of people appreciate what you do for them because they are not used to seeing things get done. For example, in every corner of India, people know what telecom is doing for them. And these are people who need help. They are the key to India's future. They have to be lifted for India to keep her head up high.

People in India do not want change. Everything seems comfortable. Don't rock the boat. They do not like people from the outside with new ideas. If you tell people to go this way, they will say no, and go that way. If you tell them to go that way, they will go this way. Basically what they are saying is: don't move.

All the change that takes place in India is incremental – small cosmetic changes made here and there. This is because people are afraid to fail. They have low self-esteem and do not try new things or take risks. As I have said before, Indians do not feel like a powerful nation of a billion people. They do not understand the power of a billion minds. And until the mindset changes, until we have the right people in positions of power who commit to building a really powerful nation, things will not change. It is fatal to go into the twenty-first century with an eighteenth or nineteenth century mindset.

India needs generational change. We have to look at a new kind of framework, in which modern thinking prevails. People have to become more inventive. Right from childhood we are conditioned to believe that we can only do this, or do that. Alternative thinking is suppressed through deep mental conditioning. In schools there is so much regimentation and discipline that at the end children actually turn out to be undisciplined, with a lack of innovation. This breeds a mentality that does not want to take risks. The idea is not that you break tradition for the sake of breaking it. But if you do not have people who challenge systems, it is impossible to bring innovations and in turn further a change in mindset. Risk taking is key to development.

It is interesting to look at how the United States has sustained its economy. I remember that during the oil crisis in the '70s, I waited in line at a gas station for an hour. In those days, many people thought that this country was going to be in deep trouble. Not only did it get out of that situation, today it has some of the lowest gas prices in the world. How do these things happen in this country? A continuous stream of people who challenge the establishment at all levels have provided the dynamics for growth in America. The country's real wealth is its mindset – the 'We can do it' mentality.

I remember one of my college professors here in America – Professor Messinger. One day he could not solve a problem in class. Immediately he said he could not seem to find the correct answer, and asked a student, John, to come on the board and solve the problem. As an Indian student I was wondering, first he says he can't solve a problem, and then he asks a student to do it. John got up and solved the problem. The professor said, "I told you. John is very smart." And he was so proud of it. I could not imagine this situation in India – the teacher would have felt humiliated if a student would solve a problem that he could not. I was stunned by the professor's level of self-esteem.

Efforts Underway

Many young people in India have tried to do new things. Some with success and others without. Hundreds of thousands have left the country – to do well in places that may be more suited for their enterprise and nature. Thousands are leaving even now, especially technology professionals. They leave for various reasons of course, one of them being that they do not find the right challenges and environment to fulfill their goals at home.

Of course, it would be foolish to think that there has been no change at all. Things have been changing rapidly with the impact of technology. Travel, communications and the media have exposed people in India to other parts of the world. They look at other countries and question how so many things have been possible there. We need an acceleration of these processes. Many more of these people have to enter politics to effect a large change in the mainstream.

I am not implying here that we should throw away our family values, relationships, religion and customs. Mindset relates to taking action, implementing new ideas and discovering a sense of determination.

Ten-point Connect

This problem of mindset directly relates us back to the each of the other points of the 10-point program – national agenda, political reforms, decentralized decision-making, population control, fulfilling basic human needs, further economic liberalization, infrastructure, institution building and human resource development. None of these can be mobilized without a change in people's mindset.

■

ON **MANAGEMENT**

I f India is full of complexities, then so is the corporate world. The idea of a company running well oiled, without incident, with employees fitting together neatly to achieve the task at hand, is an absurd concept to anyone who has ever worked even a day in business. Corporate management is a delicate process of shielding egos, making tough decisions, considering difficult ethical issues, and meeting high expectations.

This part of the book explores these complexities in detail, looking into the many managerial, human, and social challenges that emerge in the daily grind of business.

For example, businesses often grow out of very tight individual partnerships. But those partnerships are inevitably tested by the ups and downs of building an enterprise. How can these kinds of partnerships be managed? Hiring employees can also be the difference between success and failure for a business. There are important concepts to consider when hiring new people. But it's also important to discuss what happens when you have hired someone who isn't doing a good job. How does a manager make the difficult decision to lay off or invest further in an employee?

Very often management comes down to personalities. Issues like poor self esteem among employees can be the reason for an unproductive workforce. The inevitable reality of office politics can cripple a successful enterprise, if not properly managed. And these issues are never more pertinent than when a company experiences a leadership change, and a new manager is brought in. Both managers and employees always need to be working toward a common set of goals, but achieving that does not come down to just a few trite slogans and leadership concepts. It's a jungle out there.

Life as a corporate manager can be a lonely experience, with dozens of conflicting interests constantly jostling for attention. Two truths remain completely set in stone — the need to manage in an ethical manner, as well as the importance of understanding the bigger picture. Managers must remember that no matter how high they climb, they should still be grounded in real world values.

Welcome to the trenches, where we examine the inner workings of the corporate world.

■

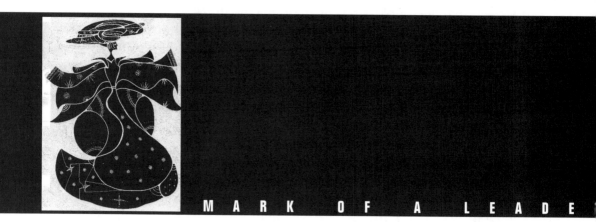

MARK OF A LEADER

As technological and economic changes sweep the world, the characteristics of a great leader change in some aspects and remain steadfast in others. Here is a snapshot of what makes (and breaks) a leader who brings about generational change- in both political and business settings.

L eadership is about *leading*, not *managing*. It is about motivating, not monitoring. In a sense, it is about *vision* and *values*. It is about making hard, bold decisions and living with those decisions through difficult times. It is about fighting against the tide. It is about listening to your gut beliefs.

Leadership starts with a vision of what you want to create, whether it is a company, nation, mission or agenda. A leader should be able to visualize, break up things into smaller, workable pieces, get people to accomplish them and thereafter, be able to put it all back together.

The second most important requirement is a set of values: virtues that span areas such as self-discipline, compassion, responsibility, courage, perseverance, honesty, loyalty, truth and absolute truth. If a leader possesses a certain true set of values, there will always be followers. A leader must practice what he/she is going to preach; otherwise there will be no followers.

Performance

For a leader to garner faith from followers, he/she must deliver performance. There is often a period of "getting up to speed," but if the performance is lacking over a period of time, people will start to look elsewhere for new leadership.

Quality of Standards

Like morality and virtue, a leader must consistently talk about, project and demand a high quality of standards. If a leader does not demand quality, the entire organization will assume that high standards are not important.

Human Skills

Because a leader constantly deals with a lot of people, he/she should be able to motivate them. Anytime you make a decision, you make some people happy and alienate others. Making a different decision will change the combination. Decisions often result in contradictions, and a leader must learn to handle them.

Time Management

Everybody wants a leader's time, exactly the thing he/she does not have a lot to spare. In a sense, the only gift that anybody can give a leader is time, and the only way to do that is by not it taking up. Messages or ideas should be conveyed in as little time and as efficiently as possible.

Stake Holders

Who are a leader's stakeholders or constituency? For corporate leaders, this group could be shareholders, employees, vendors, customers, management or others. For political leaders, it is the people – the voters. A leader has to balance the interest of the constituency with her mission and vision, while keeping her values intact. A leader has to be able to communicate the big vision to the stakeholders. He/she has to sell that vision, and never get tired of doing it. He/she must show in her vision a tremendous amount of contagious enthusiasm. If a leader cannot communicate the vision, the vision is no good.

A leader is really a cheerleader. Those around must feel charged up about the collective mission he/she sets. A leader must also have a sense of destiny, and a sense of sacrifice. As you build people up, and then let them advance smoothly, you get more out of them. If he/she rises above petty things, people are attracted to her original ideas and visions.

Communications and Media Management

In this day and age, our senses are bombarded with information and images from every quarter. Outside an organization, a local event can become international instantly. Within an organization, even minor management issues at the top level trickle down through employees of the company very quickly – often leaking out to the outside world. All this makes it important for every leader to have excellent communication skills – within the company and in outside media projections.

This is a parameter of leadership that has changed substantially over the decades. Leaders like Mahatma Gandhi mobilized the entire nation on the basis of symbols. The word "salt" energized everybody in India. This is not possible today as leaders appear on different media platforms. In a sense, this relatively new characteristic of leadership has changed the concept of leadership itself. A leader has to be able to stand calmly in front a gathering of financial analysts on Wall Street and defend the company's position, as well as be able to express the humanitarian values of the company during a social fundraiser.

At the same time, it is critical to remember that once again, the fundamental values of leadership have not changed. No amount of public savvy will work if the values are not sound. You can fool some people some of the time, but you can't fool everybody all of the time.

One Eye, Many Hands

Every organization has only one leader. The rest are managers who manage a piece of the leader's vision. There is a great buzz these days that all managers in companies should be "leaders," a concept that is just not possible! Sure, everyone has to "lead" their department and their tasks, but that's management. The vision and the values nevertheless come from the very top, from the leader. The rest are only managing that vision – conveying the message from the leader effectively. They should themselves believe in it, and be clear as to the piece of the vision that they are responsible for implementing.

Business and Political Leadership

Business and political leadership have traditionally been perceived as divergent, in terms of the characteristics of leaders in both arenas, as well as in the effect of political leadership on business and vice versa.

Needless to say, politics inevitably seeps into corporate settings – demanding that a leader have skills that are appropriate for both corporate as well as political settings. Consider the example of a manufacturing plant that needs to be relocated. Dealing with this can build up into a political situation, since many employees' lives are centered around their place of business: children and families have to be relocated, new homes and schools found, and so on. These kinds of circumstances breed power plays; a leader has to be able to handle it well, using all the skills described above.

Leadership is not about intellectual capability. A leader does not need to have knowledge in all things related to the business or policy. In fact, her ignorance is a great blessing, because that keeps the leader's mind open, enabling her to seek input from all angles and make decisions from his gut. As long as the values are sound and intact, the decisions made are in favor of the common goal.

A leader must be humble, but must have power inside, because at the end of the day leadership is all about venturing to unknown paths alone. There are lots of people following, but no one walking alongside.

Sycophants vs. Advisors

Sycophants are those who tell the leader what he/she wants to hear. Their vested interest is in promoting their agenda, as opposed to what will benefit the larger mission. They constantly try to please the leader, and not help her make hard decisions. As a result, the leader often likes sycophants. This can cause the leadership to fail in the long run.

Because of a leader's solitary position, he/she must be very careful not to have sycophants or "yes-people" around. If she falls into that trap, she will begin to listen to their voices instead of her own. This creates barriers for other viewpoints, leading to conflict. A leader must keep her ears to the ground before making decisions. When she makes important decisions, there may not be too many people who concur. But once the decision is made, she has to ensure everyone follows it.

Cultural Product

Are leaders born or are leaders made? Well, they're made, but they are a product of their environment. They do require some fundamental qualities to begin with, which are enhanced by their cultural, educational, family and professional experience.

Cultural diversity helps in building good leadership qualities because it enables one to see things from different angles. Cultural diversity brings in ideological diversity and tolerance to ethnicity. In today's corporate world, understanding different viewpoints is as important for a leader as understanding finance, marketing, strategy, sales, quality, production and performance.

A good leader always builds leaders who *can* replace him, but who *don't*. For that, a leader must always "create" people who will take charge, but make sure that the individual does not become a threat, as is often the case both in political and corporate setups. It's a very fine balance: Create your replacement, but never need to use it. That's one of the risks of being a leader!

Some leaders are agents who bring about generational change, while others usher in incremental change. The former are the real leaders. They are the ones who leave a mark, a legacy and really make a difference.

■

JUST DO IT, TOGETHER

The excitement of collaborating with like-minded people to successfully start a new company is incredible. But one vision, one drive, one idea can often crumple into conflicts, marred egos, unnecessary litigation and eventual failure. Here is what can go wrong in partnerships, and how to handle those situations.

Partnerships have been a traditional way of starting, structuring and developing businesses. Lots of technology companies are based on partnerships that bring together different talents from different groups – technology, management, finance and services. The idea, of course, is to gather a team and hope they can work together through good and bad times, until everyone's personal objectives are met and the team is ready to move on to different things. But partnerships can go awry, and relationships among relatives and friends may even get destroyed in the process. There are four main issues that are critical in making any partnership a success.

Clarity

Be clear about who is bringing what to the table, right from the beginning. Initially of course, everyone is enthusiastic and willing to contribute everything, so this type of conversation gets pushed off. Factors such as whether the partnership is equal or unequal, whether one partner is providing marketing and the other technology, should be firmly established from the beginning, and documented. Besides the mandatory shareholder agreement, very few founders actually document the roles and relationships of partners. Neglecting to do this leads to problems in perception of responsibility and other misunderstandings. As important as it is to hold periodic meetings on the business plan and growth of the company, it is important to meet to review the partner relationship as well.

Communication

This point is not about communicating on a day-to-day basis, but in a formal way. The beginning of the end of a partnership can often be traced to a lack of communication. And, bear in mind, communication problems do not occur when you promise less and deliver more; they begin when a partner promises more and delivers less, saying, "Don't worry, I'll take care of it" — but does not do so.

If communication becomes disrupted, attempt to improve communication within the partnership. Going to lawyers often results in a complete breakdown of direct communication. The key is to keep certain boundaries. For example, friendships or family matters should not be allowed to enter business. A big problem often seen in Asian business relationships is the blurring of boundaries between what is family and what is business. Often, partnerships that start off well with a great deal of understanding and good documentation, get ruined because members of one of the partners' families get involved, setting off a spiral of social politicking that may creep into the way of business, creating tensions and eventually tearing the partners apart.

For example, two of my friends started a business. At the beginning, the friendship was healthy, communication was informal and little documentation was kept. After a while, their spouses began to get involved. Positions were created for them, and the manner in which the business was run became more and more casual. One of the spouses, who handled finance, started commenting about the expenditures of others. The line between personal and business relations disappeared, and the results were catastrophic. That's why I recommend that partners communicate and keep each other updated.

Conflict Resolution

It is essential to have a planned mechanism for the resolution of conflicts. Conflicts between partners are a normal occurrence and likely to crop up over the state of the business or the mentality of the people involved. Conflicts often start when business is doing extremely well, or extremely poorly. In either case, one or more of the partners may want to bail out – in the former case, a partner may be looking to cash out, or devote more time to other things, such as his or her family life, whereas the other may want to keep working at the same, or an even harder, pace. And in the latter, a partner may be looking to get out of the mess to move on to something else. If the business is doing poorly, one person might want to bail out, and the other may want to make a go of it. Big egos and the tendency to take credit for any success can cause trouble. If one partner has a big ego, the other one has to be content to stay in the background: often times, there is not room enough for two egos in one business. Third-party intervention is critical in such cases. The neutrality of the party is also vital. I had a friend whose partner once brought his significant other into the partnership, which effectively turned every debate into a two-on-one affair, defeating the purpose of a third party.

Realization that Partnerships Do End

Many people are under the impression that a partnership will go on indefinitely – perhaps for generations. Both parties must realize that a partnership is a temporary state of affairs; it is created for a purpose — to meet a goal. After that goal has been met, the partnership will be dissolved. At the outset, the duration of the partnership should be sketched out: 3 years, 5 years, 10 years, and so on. If, in the middle of a partnership, one party wants to restructure his or her wealth, the company would be forced to restructure. By having a plan of action, partners can avoid unpleasant surprises. Partners should be able to anticipate the time period for exit plans, whether this is by selling, going public or some other strategy.

Although all partnerships start well, very few end well. Poor planning often causes friction between partners. Conflict between partners can pervade every level in a company; a crack in the leadership can result in employees taking sides. It is a rare employee that has the courage to tell the company's founders not to fight, for the benefit of the company. Instead, employees add to the conflict and take sides, depending on who they think is right, what they think happened and also who they think they can benefit from most. Siding with one partner can be a way of getting closer to the partner, eventually leading to personal gain. All these factors can cause the demise of a partnership.

A partnership, first and foremost, is about understanding the other person. Crucial to this understanding is the clarity in communication between partners. Each party should clearly state its position to the other. All too often, in Indian businesses, nepotism and the lack of demarcation between a personal and a business relationship results in chaos. By the use of proper documentation, healthy communication, firmly established conflict resolution methods and an understanding of the temporality of such ventures, partnerships can have the winning edge.

■

MANAGING RISK

Given the current, drastically different business climate, here's a discussion on a vital issue - managing risk.

M anaging risk in business has two dimensions. One is related to resources, the other is related to ecosystems.

Resources include people, products, processes and markets. We'll go into each one of these in a little more detail later. The ecosystem refers to the entire support system for the business. It includes the whole ecology, which depends on suppliers, vendors and customers.

The computer industry has its own ecosystem, and it comprises many subsystems. For example Apple's ecosystem, IBM's, Oracle's and Microsoft's. All of these feed into each other. Whenever a totally different idea appears, a paradigm shift can take place, and the ecosystem is disturbed. That creates a whole different dimension for risk.

Resources

People - First to be affected is people. In any business, people risk is a significant issue. That's because people make things happen. Companies try to minimize these risks by offering incentive packages, including bonuses. They also try to create an environment of trust, loyalty and honesty.

Products - Most of the time products are protected by intellectual property laws, whether patents, trademarks, or copyrights. Product risks can be mitigated by creating a really great R&D function headed by a visionary who looks at the competition, and at the capabilities that will be required in the future.

Processes - The third risk is process, which implies putting controls in place, implementing quality standards and performance, and cost parameters. It implies creating a system and discipline that doesn't depend too much on people.

Markets - Marketing related risk depends on the real market you're addressing. You need to perform competitive analysis and understand the market segment by segment. You need constant vigilance. This is very important in positioning your product. For instance, in emerging markets, you have political risk. Changes in political relationships will cause changes in market dynamics.

The Ecosystem

After looking at these four areas, you then map it to an ecosystem — the kind of company you are at this stage. Are you at the first phase? Are you at the expansion phase? Are you at the leadership phase? Or are you in the self-renewal phase?

A friend of mine, management consultant James Moore, did an interesting study that outlines the risk scenario. Basically, it says that at the birth of a business, the ecosystem is such that you're betting on your seed innovation - the idea that can lead to new products. You're discovering the right customer value proposition and designing a business that can sell to the market.

At this stage, your risks are different. You are enthusiastic, you know the product and you know how to make it better. You're basically hoping to change the paradigm.

Then you have to work with customers and suppliers to define the new proposition around your own innovation. Your competitive advantage is your idea. You want to protect your idea through a patent, trademark or copyright.

The ecology here is undeveloped. You don't have too many connections. Not too many outsiders know about your idea. So the risk of others stealing or copying it and such is very little.

Then you get into the expansion phase. The ecology again changes completely. Now you bring the new offering to market. You work with more suppliers and partners. You scale up the operation to increase market coverage. Now your competition, and thus the risks, are probably very different. You try to standardize. You ask other people to use the same product. You reach out to a large number of people.

Then you take on the leadership role. You need to provide vision to everybody - suppliers, customers and vendors. You have to encourage your suppliers and customers to work together, to continue to improve your offering. Then your risks change, because your supplier may come up with a better idea. At this point you have to maintain a bargaining position and power in relation to other players in the ecosystem. Otherwise, they will eat your space.

Finally, there is self-renewal. You work with other innovators to bring new ideas into the ecosystem. Somebody else comes to you with an innovation. Or you, as a leader, can acquire little companies. You don't need to invent anything.

That's how big companies maintain a high barrier to entry. They create a huge ecosystem of their own. This keeps other innovators from building new, competitive ecosystems. All the necessary relationships are in place. For some other guy to do that would be a huge investment of time, energy, money and people.

The Matrix
Evaluating risk in one area is not good enough. It's a huge, complex matrix.

You need to understand what phase of development you're in. That dictates how you view risk. Take the example of Apple, Intel, Microsoft and IBM — four different ecosystems. How do they manage risk?

In its early days, when Apple was building its ecosystem, IBM had the big muscle. IBM decided to enter the PC market, and basically ran with the show. That created an ecosystem for Microsoft automatically. Then, knowing that IBM was becoming too powerful in the PC business, Microsoft and Intel joined hands. There was a time when IBM invested in Intel, because it was using Intel processors instead of its own.

The lesson to learn is that you have to be constantly aware of your ecology.

Projecting Risk

Communication is a key part of managing risk. Employees must be told constantly about risk. They must know that if they don't deliver in a certain time period, someone else will. If the product is not improved, someone else will grab market share. If costs are not reduced, there will be loss of business. There must be constant focus on creating value for customers.

To the outside world, however, all of these things are turned around and presented as a benefit. The company makes a better product with higher performance, lower cost and better service. What is seen as a challenge inside must be seen as an opportunity by the outside world.

As a startup, you have to run at 100 miles an hour, while being constantly vigilant. There's no shortcut, and that's a significant risk factor too. Intensity and energy have to be extremely high. That's the only way you can succeed - because others are putting the same amount of energy into it. If you don't, it won't happen for you. You need to constantly evaluate risk and understand it has many dimensions. There are no shortcuts, no simple formula to managing risk. It's an ongoing, full-time activity. You can't take it lightly when building a business.

■

MANAGING MEDIOCRITY

In a corporate environment, especially in the high-tech industry, knowledge-based workers are the key to the future. They are the most critical aspect of business productivity. But we all have different skill sets. Motivation, intelligence, education, understanding, expectations, enthusiasm and discipline, all vary from person to person. As a result, you always find a few in the group who are mediocre - the below-average performers.

Mediocre employees don't really deliver what's expected of them. They don't realize, appreciate or accept that they are not really performing. They are somehow difficult to manage. In fact, they are on the verge of being incompetent because they can't do things right. You give them a job, spend time explaining it, and when it comes back to you in the end it won't be right.

They are more form than substance. They talk more about procedures and formalities. Sometimes you'll ask them a question and they'll come back with more questions. They are not driven by their lights. They hardly deliver on time. They cannot complete tasks as outlined. Somehow they're not good at details. Mediocrity is reflected in spelling mistakes, forgetting to put dates, page numbers, signatures. The lack of accuracy, misunderstanding, and miscommunication are all bound together. You know the type. Every organization must deal with these people.

But you have to be careful. People within the same organization will have different personalities. You have to see each person's good part, and work on the bad part.

Somebody may be highly motivated but perhaps not have the skill set. Somebody with the skill set is perhaps not motivated. These also are not mediocrity problems. You must decide how to work on these people. Then you have to say, "Look, you don't put in enough energy. You don't come in on time. You don't listen. You don't write well. You don't check your numbers." In other words, be very specific.

Temperament and ego problems can also affect people. You have to let these people know that others have come forward with perceptions of an ego problem. Something might be said along the lines of, "I know you're a great guy, but let's work on it. You don't need to get uptight about showing your ego to everybody. We need to emphasize teamwork to get the job done, but it appears that your ego is getting in the way. I know you don't mean that. I know that's not the signal you want to send, but this is what everybody is feeling. So can we work on it? It's in your interest and my interest, and it's in the interest of the company."

It's not very easy to have these dialogues. That's why the manager has to practice it. The manager has to make sure that he doesn't get personal in thinking. That's where maturity comes in.

Dealing with Mediocrity in the Corporate World

But what if the problem really is mediocrity? There are basically two options when dealing with mediocrity in a business. Someone who is doing far less than perfect can be replaced with someone who is better, but it often takes a lot more time to hire someone new, and then you don't know how the new person is going to work.

The other option is to keep the person, train him, and somehow work with him to bring his performance to a level that's accepted. That's what we want to really discuss. How do you do that? It is indeed a very difficult task.

Begin a Dialogue

The first and foremost thing to do is begin a dialogue. For this, a manager or supervisor really has to prepare and practice, even if it means writing down what to say, when to say it and how to say it. In the meeting, start with positive things, like the person's personality, or communication skills. But then it's time to get into where the improvements need to be made.

You might say, "Hey, look, you need to improve. We're going to talk about your improvements." It should be explicitly mentioned to him in terms of, "Hey, I'm really not here to criticize you; I'm here to help you improve your work performance. I would like you to listen, and do things as we agree, and I want you to ask questions. I want you to really focus on quality at work. Do things right the first time, review things before you submit them to supervisors or me, and look at the format of the documents or the task."

You can then explain, "The best way to do that, according to me as a manager/supervisor, is to decide what steps we're going to take between us. I'd like to do little things first. Let's not worry about the big picture. Let's take baby steps.

"The next task I give you is one of the small baby steps we're going to take. Then, we'll jointly work out a timetable, no more than 90 days, to review periodically. Then we'll decide at the end of 90 days, collectively, if your skill set has improved, or not. We are not talking about you improving. We're talking about your skill set improving."

I think it's very important to say that. This first meeting is really critical in terms of confronting the individual. Basically, in a sense, to say, "Hey look, you're mediocre. You're not doing your job well. I'm not happy with you. But we're going to work together to improve your skill set. We'll review it, but for that we need to take baby steps."

Avoid Isolation

The second item, having done this discussion and dialogue and the critical meeting, is to recognize that this person cannot be isolated, or cut off from any meeting or group discussion. You've got to then make a special effort to give importance to this individual, to build his self-esteem, which to some extent you may have hurt. Even though you've said, "I'm not criticizing you, I'm criticizing your work," he's not going to be able to distinguish that. In group meetings, try to praise him. Boost his morale. And whenever he shows good results, compliment him. Keep him involved in many more meetings. Show an example of his good work to others.

Continue the Dialogue
The third thing is to really continue the dialogue and review all of the baby steps, once a week at first, then once every two weeks. The 90 days you've laid out should be structured properly. You don't want to come back at the end of 90 days and say, "Okay, it's time to review."

Be a Mentor
The fourth thing is to be a supporter, teacher or friend. He should feel that you are genuinely interested in his improvement, and that he needs to improve for you, as well as for him. Through this, he's going to be a better person and better performer, and you will have shown the desire to help. It's important for everyone involved to realize that this is teamwork toward improvement. If necessary, send the person to an outside training class. Then he'll feel this is a reward.

When the 90 Days Are Up
At the end of the 90-day period, it's time to decide if the employee has improved. Once you've decided, set up the final meeting. This is the time to fire him or not. The manager has to be bold and bite the bullet, if it's needed. If you don't do what needs to be done at the end of 90 days, you're not doing justice to the company or the employee. After 90 days, if no improvement is seen, it's time to invest in another person and let him go.

If, on the other hand, you see continued improvement, then you'll know that you've succeeded together. You've then lifted the standard and quality of this person. He becomes an asset, as opposed to a liability, of the company.

Avoid Emotion
This is how I've dealt with mediocrity. I've had to work with many mediocre people in my career. And, as I've noted above, you can't get angry with them,

because ultimately you need to get work done through others. You can't do everything yourself. As a result, you have to really lay out a plan like this, and deal with it. Most of the time, managers don't like to confront this kind of a situation, but if you hide it, or ignore it, it won't go away.

The key, in both meetings, is not to get very emotional. Don't start pointing fingers as in, "You didn't do this, you didn't do that, that's not right," etc. That's counterproductive. It doesn't communicate what you want to communicate. You don't want to communicate frustration. You want to communicate concern.

Sometimes it also helps to have the person do a spot-analysis of himself, sit down and really discuss it. If he realizes that the boss is ready to work with him, he will also change. It's all common sense, but not many people do that.

Handling Mediocrity Down The Chain of Command

The president has to make sure that his group does the same. Everybody in the group has to follow the same format. It has to be done at the lowest possible level. So the lower supervisor has to make sure that there's no mediocrity. But your supervisor reports to managers. Managers have to make sure that none of the supervisors are mediocre. It's the same hierarchical format.

Articulating the Vision

One final point about performance and the corporate vision. Leaders really have to constantly articulate their wishes to the group that, in turn, must work toward fulfilling those wishes, and that vision. The group has to feel it is working for a company that it wants to build. Whatever the vision is, it has to be outlined loudly and clearly. That way, people will realize it when they don't fit into the vision. They'll know they're all working toward building a company that does this, this, this and this.

There are role models, there is competition — this is how we improve quality. This is how we beat the competition. This is how we make money. That's what it really is all about.

■

MAKING OFFICE POLITICS WORK FOR YOU

Politics in the workplace is inevitable. Ignoring it causes significant damage. But if dealt with skillfully, it can be used to serve the larger corporate agenda of the company.

P olitics is very much a part of every human organization, whether it be in the family, nonprofit organizations, government agencies or, especially, in the corporate world. In fact, when there are more than three people working together, politics is inevitable. Corporate politics affects people and performance, and, as a result, profits. It eventually becomes a serious issue when it hurts employee morale.

Corporate politics springs essentially from conflicts between the corporate agenda, the group agenda and an individual's agenda. Whenever people try to advance their own agenda into the mainstream, politics looms.

In the corporate world, the highest element is the board of directors. Each director brings to the table different backgrounds and different experiences, and thus a different perspective. When they feel strongly about a particular agenda, they begin to lobby other directors. That is the seed of corporate politics.

From the board, the politicking moves down to the executive team — CEO, COO, CFO, CTO — and ultimately, reaches managers and individual workers. In addition, pockets of politics exist in different sectors of the organization. Politics also relates to the egos of strong personalities who lobby for a personal agenda and create an environment that hurts others. Gossip starts, tension is created, people become fearful and unsure whose side to take or what to say. They worry about their jobs, their security, and their pay. "Who will win? Will I survive?" they ask.

Open Communication

What does it take to deal with, manage and minimize corporate politics? How do you really create good politics so that together you move the corporate agenda, rather than the individual agenda, forward? The starting point in dealing with corporate politics is to grasp and accept that politics is part of corporate culture. There's nothing wrong with it. It's there, and you can't get rid of it, so you have to really make the best of it.

Secondly, it is important to deal with it. The best way to deal with it is to create open communication channels at all levels. The company vision needs to be articulated from the top, time and time again. It needs to be taught in public, open forums such that people get a sense of direction and the objective toward which everyone is supposed to work.

In today's environment, where technology is critical and knowledge is so important, open communication among knowledge workers is critical. Traditional factory jobs are defined clearly. The knowledge element is tiny for people stamping something at a workstation or handling a machine. So, corporate politics diminishes in those situations. In the knowledge industry, however, many workers apply brainpower. As a result, there is much more room for politics. That makes it imperative to capitalize on openness and good communication. By articulating the company vision periodically, management gives people the feeling that they know their objectives.

Identifying Power Centers

Another consideration in dealing with corporate politics is recognizing organizational power centers. Who — or what — really wields power in or over the firm? Is it within the management structure, or outside — perhaps someone on the board or in a vendor company, or a customer? When the company's not doing well, the power center may even shift to a financial institution. Then the banker and his political agenda, become very critical. Once you recognize where the power centers are, and what their agenda is, you can begin to understand politics.

Alignment Of Agendas

Third, it is necessary to align the power center's agenda with the corporate agenda, as much as possible. If that can't be done, you have to confront it. Some employees use corporate politics in the wrong way. There must be open communication with them. Confront them if it's consistently negative. Say, "Look, this behavior is not helping our company. Before you go up against each other, let's talk about it. What are you trying to achieve? How does it help you?"

You have to try to manage it before it becomes too big of a problem in the company. Hiding it, avoiding it, or ignoring it is not the answer.

If you, as CEO or manager, ignore politics in your group or in your company, you'll be seen as a weak member of the team. As a result, power centers sprout away from where the power really belongs. Pockets of power emerge in an organization, based on what is important at that point in time. If, for example, technology is important while you're developing a product, power centers will emerge among technology people. And once the product is built, they may shift toward marketing, customer service and quality, among other areas. And power centers move as a company grows. In a mature company, power centers are found in operations. But they can shift depending on whether a company is prospering or not. And, as noted above, they can migrate outside of the company.

If a company is not doing well, is being sold, or merged or filing for Chapter II, all kinds of politics spring up as rumors start and people panic. And that lowering of morale lowers the value of the company. When you're not doing well, the downslide must be managed properly, or it will move very fast. That's why it's important for a CEO to be on top of corporate politics all the time and know who the political people are.

Managing Conflict

Some employees, after all, are more in tune with politicking than with performance. They may have important jobs within the organization, yet politics is in their character. The job of leadership is to identify these people and work with them. For others, however, corporate politics is frustrating. "Why should we have corporate politics?" they ask. "Why can't we just do our work?"

Unfortunately, that's not possible. In group dynamics, where large numbers of people are involved, people inevitably clash, because of personalities or egos or agendas. Managing conflict in this situation becomes very critical.

To me, there's nothing wrong with corporate politics, as long as you make the best of it by directing the energy toward building a positive force within the company and achieving the larger corporate agenda. It's a tough task for management, but it can be done. In fact, it has to be done.

∎

PEOPLE AS PRODUCTS

People make businesses happen. Every executive has his or her ways to hire and fire people. Yet there are a few fundamental, simple home rules that are overlooked by both the employer and the newly hired.

When Rockefeller was asked what business he was in, he answered, "I'm in the business of hiring good people." Whenever you ask venture capitalists what they invest in, almost invariably the answer is: "We invest in the right people. If the right people are involved, they will make sure that the product and the technology turns out to be right." If the wrong people are involved, even with the right product, they will mess it up. Sure, everyone recognizes that people are the key asset to a business; but employers still pay very little attention to hiring.

How to hire, whom to hire and when to hire – this is more of an art than a science. How do you tell a good employee from a bad one? A potential success from a potential failure? How do you define good chemistry? When you hire someone, you are not simply hiring him or her to work in isolation; they must fit into a system, a culture that in turn would be suitable to take the business forward. How do you begin this process?

The Start

The starting point is to identify exactly what you are looking for. Very few managers spend enough time doing this – clarifying their own thoughts about what they need to achieve by hiring someone. It is a good idea to answer a few questions in writing, like: Why do you need to hire people right now? What would be the new employee's role, responsibility and relationships? Who will they work for, who will they report to, and who will they work with? Essentially, this is like writing a product specification. After all, hiring can be equated to shopping around for a very specific product.

Outside agencies (headhunters), are often very effective in getting the right person for the job. They have systems and processes in place that enable them to do that. They ask employers what they are looking for from potential candidates, forcing them to create that product specification sheet. There are so many different elements in the selection process – personality, communication skills, teamwork skills, self-esteem, positive outlook, strong work ethic, education, experience, honesty, loyalty, reliability, sincerity, commitment and enthusiasm. But ultimately, it often comes down to simple eye contact with the person across the table. Sometimes you can look into the eye of the person and you know that they are the right one for the job, even though you may not know why. And if this chemistry is not right, no matter what the expertise, there are sure to be conflicts. Thus, the selection process should include as many co-workers and managers as possible, so that besides you, others in the organization who are going to work with a prospective candidate may contribute to this process.

When writing specs for a headhunter or for your own internal search committee, be sure to include notes about the environment and culture of your company – to paint a picture of the general atmosphere in which this person will contribute. Even with all the technical qualifications, if a potential employee is not going to mesh well with the group, everyone is headed for trouble.

In startups of course, employers look for co-workers among their professional and personal circle of friends; in larger companies, headhunters are used. Either way, you are looking for a trained, proven product, so that this hired person does not learn at your cost, and deliver later. After all, you are hiring someone to do the job now, not a year from now.

Once you have a short list of two or three candidates, do background checks. These days, people tend to exaggerate their contribution to previous projects – and resumes and interviews often reveal an inflated self-evaluation.

Personal to Professional

Here is how I go about interviewing people. This has worked for me; it may or may not work for others. I begin by talking about what we are and what we are trying to do – the company, business, philosophy, background and environment. Then I ask the candidate to tell a similar story, starting from childhood – something about their time growing up. Then we discuss the candidate's education, work experience and current job. This is often followed by a discussion of how the company's and candidate's experiences and goals may complement one another. To some, this sequence may seem to be reversed, but to me, commitment to work and responsibility comes out loud and clear when one talks about personal life.

For interviewees, it is very critical to be honest. As far as I am concerned, I would rather hear someone say honestly, for instance, that they are looking to get some experience for two to three years before moving on to bigger things, than to lie and say that they are looking to make a long career with this company.

Move!

Career change is a way of life. People must change tracks. The concept of a 30 to 40-year career with one company is over. Once you have decided to change careers, be honest about the fact that you have no experience in the new line, but you are determined to give it your best shot to do well. This honesty is often respected, and can land you right where you want to be.

And do not go overboard on education; it is not necessarily important beyond a point in life. Education basically helps you do two things: think independently and recognize that learning is a lifelong process that never ends. Once this is understood, further degrees of education lose significance, and character, attitude and enthusiasm take the center-stage in life and work.

General Pointers

When my son Salil decided to take his first job, he asked me for some guidance. At that time I wrote a list of pointer for him, some general and some personal. These are all simple human messages, but we lose track of them. Here are 10 general pointers that can be applied to anyone in any work situation.

Focus on the Job at Hand: it is your first job – new people, new city, new processes, new priorities. Do not mix business and personal/pleasure agenda. Capitalize on opportunity – this is your first step to the future, be work-centric

Develop Discipline: Be up early, on time to the office and late to leave. Sleep, eat and dress well. Attend to no personal calls/agenda. Be serious and friendly. Do not take long lunches or coffee breaks. The devil is in the details – follow up. Say what you mean and mean what you say.

Maintain a Positive Attitude: be positive. Carry energy and enthusiasm. Be willing to do extra. Remain humble, smart, low-key, hardworking and good at follow up and details. Possess a "can-do," get-things-done mentality. Take initiative and do not wait for directions.

Be a Team Player: no egos. Keep high-esteem, for self and others. Be ready to help others. Listen well. Be ready to take notes and play multiple roles. Be open, honest and truthful.

Develop Leadership: Take charge of meetings (agenda, time, objectives and notes). Exhibit larger concerns. Be sensitive to deliverables – who will do what when? Anticipate problems before they happen. Communicate well (slow and very organized). Loyalty is key.

Understand Corporate Roles and Relationships: understand corporate power and politics – what drives each player. Realize the difference in personal agendas vs. corporate goals, doers vs. front line people, form vs. substance.

Try New Ideas and Innovations: think out of the box. Ask questions never asked. Do not take no for an answer. Question fundamentals. Take risks.

Integrate Disciplines: integration of resources and perceptions. Know that technology, marketing and finance always go hand in hand. Time is an expensive resource.

Focus on Business Fundamentals: this is basic to your success. Why/What is this business? Investments, assets, liabilities, profit/loss, cash flow, financials. Products, markets, legal. Competition, price, production, quality. Human resources. Strategy. Purpose, priority, plan, process, price.

Keep an Eye on the Long Term Goals: lessons learned from each assignment. Keep a personal file on cases – people/projects. How can we benefit? How do corporations waste resources? Why do businesses get into trouble? Why do they succeed? Keep an open mind to new experiences.

Specific Pointers

Do These Everyday: Focus on difficult jobs early in the day. Keep routine work for the afternoon. Schedule important meetings at 9:00 a.m. Learn to manage time. List five to 10 items everyday to do the next day.

Weekly Self-Review: Review your accomplishments. Chart next week's agenda. Review lessons learned

Monthly Review and Reflection: Evaluate plan vs. performance. Chart plans for next month | Appraise lessons learned. Meet with boss to review: How is my performance? Do I need to improve in specific areas? Invite guidance!

Develop Communication Skills: Listen and speak. Participate in meetings. Prepare presentations, reports, graphs/charts. Keep memos.

Take Care of Health: eat right – less red meat. Exercise regularly. Drink tea, not coffee and a glass of wine, not beer

Prepare Personal Documentation: File business cards by areas and projects. Maintain project files and article clippings. Gather management tips. Learn to file and organize. Build personal organizer

Read Everyday: Wall Street Journal, business magazines, management magazines and book reviews

Learn to Invest: Join investment clubs. Know about tech stocks, major funds and growth. Look for stock market trends and emerging market trends. Understand financial instruments and event oriented investments.

Keep Track of Your Finances/Accounts: Earn, spend. Don't forget to save and analyze finances. Know how to improve them. Build assets and reduce waste. Monitor expense reports.

Enjoy Life: Work hard and play hard. Wine, dine and go to theaters, clubs, and movies. Get into fashion, partying and music. Be in touch with friends and family!

■

SELF-ESTEEM: THE INTANGIBLE YET CRITICAL WORKPLACE INGREDIENT

In modern times, more than any other time in history, self-esteem is an extremely critical aspect of work and business. The importance of self-esteem in today's workplace goes beyond psychiatrists' and social scientists' traditional view of it. The following is an examination of it using the broad context of business management in today's world.

S elf-esteem can be defined as inner strength. It is your measure of yourself. It is about belonging, being comfortable in different situations, and valuing yourself.

In general, Indians have rather fragile self-esteem and tend to get hurt very easily. Examples may sound like: "You did not invite me to your party;" "You said hello to somebody else in the morning, but not to me;" "I feel insulted and let down – you are not respecting me." In Indian mythology too, there are numerous portrayals of the "swammaan," or inner pride, being hurt.

During meetings in India in private companies, and even more in the government, strong hierarchical behavior exists, which is directly related to self-esteem. Subordinates hesitate at risking 'improper' social actions with their superiors, attempting to protect their own self-esteem. When tea is served, for example, no one in the room begins drinking until the head of the meeting commences. Whether this behavior is out of respect for the senior individual or for the sake of following the hierarchical system, it is wrongly aimed at insuring that the self-esteem of everyone in the meeting remains intact.

All modern business requires team effort; and all teamwork requires team members to respect each other. In other words, teamwork demands that knowledge is respected regardless of age, title and hierarchy. It also demands that individual members maintain a strong and stable sense of self-esteem, which is not easily shaken with disagreeable or unpleasant work assignments.

In India and in Latin America, high-asset family-run businesses, such as manufacturing or mining, face serious management problems when they try to get into a high-technology business like IT or telecom. One of these problems is management style – the inevitable adjustment that comes with the shift from a few people making all the decisions to an environment with more people working with knowledge and not requiring orders from hierarchies. Another problem with traditional work culture is that it involves high confidentiality and very little openness and access to management. In a high-tech business environment, everything is out in the open. This creates self-esteem conflicts within traditional management personnel, because they feel threatened when the high-tech worker asks probing questions concerning finance, marketing or corporate strategy.

Psychiatrists have been hired by large corporations to study and work with Asian employees who felt they were not getting the dues, recognition or promotions that they deserved. The root of these problems was nailed down to self-esteem. These workers felt that their largely Caucasian American bosses did not pat their backs enough. The bosses felt that these professionals had carried out their duties as required very accurately and that no extra recognition was necessary. Perhaps the workers were simply looking for some praise to raise their self-esteem a bit.

Social Extensions

This self-esteem issue also extends to social immigrant settings too. In the early days, at Indian parties in America, discussions on what type of immigrant status one had – student visa, work visa, permanent residency or citizenship – were common. Or people might have talked about their living arrangements – does one live in an apartment, or town home or house. The focus of these conversations would often shift to involve the various personalities as individuals lost objectivity and began to concentrate on hierarchies instead. In these environments, there was a frantic search for applause and approval.

Often in India, people come to visit others with no obvious agenda. When asked why, they say they are visiting to "pay respects." While this practice may seem like a waste of everyone's time, it is soon evident that the visitors are attempting to establish contact with a higher level – thereby increasing their self-esteem. By doing this, they enhance their personal social circle and can boast about the higher-ups they know and spend time with.

The way one is raised also directly affects his/her self-esteem. In traditional Indian families, for example, from her birth a woman is considered "paraya dhan," or someone else's wealth. Until her marriage, her family treats her as if she belongs to her future in-laws, as if she will soon marry and go away. However, once with her in-laws, she is essentially an intruder and accepted by them only when she delivers a baby boy. She has then "arrived," and her self-esteem rises.

Typically, as the child grows up in India, the family does not openly praise him or her in an attempt to avoid "spoiling" them. In America, though, children receive praise for small achievements – tying their shoelaces, carrying their school bag or finishing potty training, and so on. These little praises add to the self-esteem of the child, which have a strong influence on his or her later life.

Workplace Ethic

Self-esteem is essential for productive work because it makes workers feel comfortable, calm and cool, enabling them to focus on the task at hand, and not on trivial little things that may make them feel uncomfortable if their self-esteem is low.

Most people are reluctant to try new things when their self-esteem is at a low point. The act of trying may lead to failure, thereby proving that the person is not capable and thus embarrassing him or her. In America, self-esteem usually runs high, and this makes people more willing to attempt and achieve new things. For this reason, America is one of the more innovative countries in the world. Workers devote themselves to greater teamwork and efficiency rather than wasting their time on other matters. Self-esteem is an important parameter in building bridges with co-workers. It is a share-and-share-alike process as one person helps another with confidence and vice-versa. Team-building efforts improve greatly as workers become more conscious of each other's self-esteem and try to help maintain it. This creates better work performance and enhances leadership.

Entrepreneurs usually have high self-esteem. They leave good salaries and comfortable positions to spend their time and energy to make a dream become a reality. Their innovative approach to financial freedom puts them in control of their destiny and ensures a stable, high self-confidence.

Awareness

The first step in tackling a potential self-esteem problem is to become aware of it. Avoid making constant comparisons between yourself and others. Try to be more naturally sensitive to the needs of people around you, especially the younger ones, so that you do not appear arrogant and insulting. This will make people more comfortable with you, and allow them to perform their best.

Immigrant women, perhaps more than men, often face the most serious self-esteem problems. People have standard images of foreign women – they tend to judge by dress or appearance. The solution is to lower expectations. Expectation is blindness. When you do not expect anything, your self-esteem and your productivity are at their highest.

■

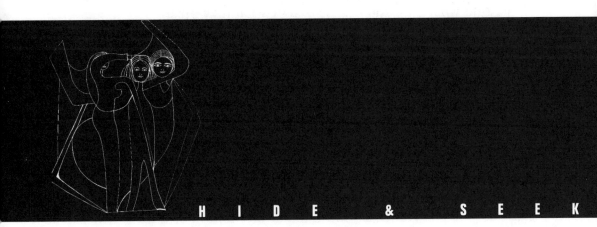

HIDE & SEEK

People often don't say what they mean, and just as often don't mean hat they say. Hidden agendas, a deep-rooted, largely cultural problem needs to be deftly handled by all concerned.

Hidden agendas is a very common phenomenon in business and social settings alike. People often have two goals that they may want to discuss, articulate, expose and convey: the idea that they communicate on the surface, which may be very different from their real purpose that they ultimately want to disclose. In the process, they want to feel you out, test the waters, buy time and judge your reaction . . . then position themselves properly to disclose the real agenda at a time when it will have an optimal reception.

In business, not focusing on the real issues may waste a great deal of time, money and resources. One needs to develop the ability to find the hidden agenda early, using perception and prediction. In Indian business or political circles especially, if someone sets up a meeting to discuss an issue related to policy, they may actually want to discuss finance. When they come, all the things they say on the surface are very different from what they mean because their body language communicates a totally different agenda. What is spoken vs. the unspoken, the openly mentioned vs. the closely held, the visible vs. the invisible, is different from what unfolds over a period of time during discussions. And what they don't say is exactly what they mean.

Sadhus and Russians

Let me give some examples. Once, while I was the chairman of the Telecom Commission of India, there were several *sadhus* (ascetics) who had been trying to see me for several weeks. So an appointment was fixed, and in walked five *sadhus* in saffron robes into my office. One of them was carrying a plastic briefcase, and as soon as I saw that, I realized that they had a hidden agenda. The leader of the bunch said to me, "A great vision reflects in your eyes." That confirmed my notion about the agenda. So I folded my hands in respect and asked them what I could do for them. They said, "Oh, nothing. We just came to pay our respects." More small talk followed, during which I kept doing my regular work, pretending to listen to them, and waiting for the real agenda to be revealed. When that didn't happen for over 20 minutes, I asked them earnestly to tell me what they wanted. "Nothing," they maintained. I tried to end the tribulation by getting up and announcing that I had to go for a meeting. They stopped me, and then the chief indicated to the *sadhu* with the briefcase and out came two pieces of paper. As it turned out, they wanted two telephone connections to their temple. I was shocked! I asked them why they didn't tell me right away – if they had, the job would have been done by then. A temple is a public place, and granting phone connections there would certainly be useful. The chief *sadhu* said, "But how could we come directly to you and openly ask you for two telephone connections!"

The message from the *sadhus* was clear. That's how these things are done in India. In my interactions with Russian bureaucrats, I found that they feel very comfortable with Indian bureaucrats and vice versa, but neither were comfortable with American bureaucrats. This is because Indians and Russians always like to dance around the issues. The goal is: never come to the point too early, or say the things that they really need to say. American bureaucrats are typically open and say things outright in a direct, conversational style that the Indians are often not equipped to handle. I find that in the American culture and business practices, though there certainly are people with hidden agendas, professionals involved in fast-moving industries are very direct and don't have too many hidden agendas.

In day-to-day work, hidden agendas create lot of confusion. In the process of answering to hidden motives, people end up misleading and hurting people, relationships get damaged because people feel they are being lied to. One needs to learn to spot those people whose work is buttering people up and exaggerating their admiration. Once you have established individual styles revealing of those you work with, you can develop multipliers – that is, each time an exaggerator says something, "divide it by three," since he or she is always over-stating things after twisting them to a certain degree. Or, if a person is low-key or conservative, "multiply by five." The art in management is developing your own scale regarding different individuals.

Predicting Accurately

To make accurate predictions, you need to ask some fundamental questions at the time of the interaction with the given person – who is he, where is he coming from, why is he saying what he is saying, how is he saying it, how much is he saying about it, how does it fit into your own agenda? Depending on your position, whether you're in marketing, management, technology, finance, whether you're a CEO, VP or project manager, you have to instantly judge how this person's work relates to yours. Does he want to join you in your mission or distract you, divert your attention or derail it? Does he wish to impose a new agenda on you? What is the person's body language saying? Why is he meeting you today – why not last week or next week? What "event" has been created to present this? These are all very complicated issues, but if you aren't able to play this game you'll end up wasting a lot of time.

Look for the "punch line" — it may or may not be verbal, it may not appear until the person's closing statements, or it may not appear at all . . . but it's up to you to find the key message. Important as it is, especially in countries like India, it is surprising that somehow this subject gets very little attention in the management schools.

Dodging Game

Former Prime Minister of India, Rajiv Gandhi once said that his biggest problem is people taking 30 minutes to say what can be said in 5. Businesspeople going to India inevitably face this problem from both ends: people dealing with them having hidden agendas, and people they deal with expect them to have hidden agendas. The trick is to remain straight and direct, yet keep a vigilant eye on pinpointing the problem and finding ways to successfully circumvent it – all without losing the mind.

A classical work situation that brings along plenty of hidden agendas is when employees ask for a raise. If an employee is seeking an unplanned, unscheduled meeting, the timing of which coincides with a performance appraisal or a raise, the employee is probably going to ask for a raise. Hidden agendas are also a reason why there are far fewer mergers, acquisitions and partnerships in India than in the US. Executives are hesitant to disclose what they really have in mind. They spend more efforts trying to fathom what's on the mind of the party across the table, than exploring avenues to work together. These efforts invariably don't lead anywhere except pseudo-competition and missed opportunities.

Culture and Personality

In the United States, being direct is respected. Because this is not the case in India, things often take a lot more time to get accomplished. In India, people are offended by directness because they are not used to it. On a social level, it is again a reflection of the feudal and hierarchical mindset that I have talked about in previous articles. On a personal level, it represents a lack of self-esteem.

While there are those that walk and talk with their hidden agendas, there are also those who expect everyone to have them. These are individuals who don't like to deal with issues without irrelevant, drawn-out preambles. Here again, cultural and personality traits come into play. These people also have low self-esteem, since they may like an ego boost before they come to address an important issue.

New Technologies Get to the Bottom

Electronic communications is more direct than verbal communications, striking hard at hidden agendas. Instead of wasting hours of time in meetings or phone conversations, its often more appropriate to review written proposals, or "converse" over email. These enable multitasking, excellent record keeping of 'conversations', and help get to the bottom of an issue quickly. At the same time although email can be a very helpful tool, different styles of writing and tone can cause serious misunderstandings.

When people come to the US from India, with their legacy of hidden agendas, they need to be nicely told that commensurate with progressive trends, they must learn to be direct. They must say what they mean and mean what they say. That is how they will be assimilated more meaningfully into the global society.

■

TACKLING REALITY HEAD-ON: DOWNSIZIN

In times of growth, cash is available for the future. But that's not the case now. People have t take a hard, realistic look at their businesses and make difficult belt-tightening decisions. Th result - downsizing.

Ten years of unprecedented growth in the American economy have created the impression, especially among young people in the high tech industry, that growth is permanent. After all, many have never seen an economic downturn, at least during their professional careers. Now the high-tech industry is going through difficult times. The stock market is down, venture capital funding is tight, private companies are struggling for cash, shutting their doors, watching their CEOs quit.

Unemployment is up, families are being forced to relocate — overall, it is a rather depressing environment compared to a few years ago. The bad news forces us to rethink the growth strategies of the past and to focus on survival strategies for the future. What matters is the speed of hard decision-making with focus and objectivity. People need to stay grounded in reality and not succumb to hype about the future.

The Four Sides of Downsizing

There are four main areas to focus on in downsizing a company. Each is interconnected. And the goal is to maximize returns:

Cash Flow Management

In today's environment, burn-rate has to be decreased and companies have to return to basics. The money coming in has to be more than the money going out. This is especially true for companies that have been spending cash received from private or public markets without ramping up their revenues. Suddenly, they have to focus on generating cash! The normal practice is to slash expenses, reduce staff, and spend less on capital equipment, office space and travel. The idea is to borrow, while building cushions and focus on financial management. The key is to not delay the hard financial decisions. In any organization, even under normal circumstances, 15 to 20 percent of expenses can be trimmed without hurting anything. But in this crisis, the focus ought to be to cut 50 percent and see if you can still survive.

Cash flow management also means looking at revenue generating possibilities that have never been seen before. During prosperous times, a company can spend time and money developing new or better products for wider markets. But that way of working only delays revenue generation. Companies may instead have to focus on products for smaller markets that generate immediate cash, which includes selling new services.

Corporate Restructuring

Companies need to restructure to reflect the realities of the changing economy and the market. This means reducing the budget and cutting the size and the ambitions of the company. Sometimes, it is better to condense the target market. Instead of looking at global markets, focus on local markets. Thus, restructuring implies re-examining the product portfolio and marketing plan while preserving the character of the company. This may also mean laying out a good media strategy to change the public perception of the company and help people understand that the company is facing difficult times. But it should not reflect the change in the market being addressed, or the core competencies.

When restructuring, relationships with banks, customers, vendors, and others, become very important. It is crucial to have clear and effective communications with all concerned, once the tactics are chosen — i.e., layoffs, reductions in product portfolio, or delayed payments to vendors. This reduces the possibility of rumors, which often lead to bad morale among all associated with the company and, in turn, reduced productivity.

Redefining Markets

These are the times to examine product revenues and profits. Focusing on higher margin products releases resources and focuses energy and capital. With companies across the board having excess inventory, it may be time to revisit suppliers and shop for better deals on components and services for products.

Similar restructuring may be required in the area of marketing. One possibility is to reduce marketing staff and take on more agents and representatives who will work on commission, something that may be hard to find in good times. The idea is to make effective use of excess manpower that the market conditions have made available outside the company. People on the street may be willing to work extra hard to produce results, on your terms and conditions, without being a cash burden on you. Part of realigning markets is looking more carefully at merger and partnership possibilities.

Readjusting Manpower

This is the most difficult aspect of downsizing. Today, 30 to 40 percent or more of business costs are related to human resources. Thus, reducing manpower is the major component of cutting costs. Cutting manpower also brings down expenses associated with travel, phones, taxes, insurance and office space. Unfortunately, it is very difficult to tell people that they are no longer needed. It requires excellent people management skills. Helping them find a new job, giving support while they look for a job, providing letters of recommendation, helping during their family crisis — all of this requires special skills and open communications. It is relatively easy to hire. But firing separates the men from the boys in human resource development.

Downsizing human resources must start at the top. You can't have a top-heavy organization when downsizing. Sometimes, top management that stays may have to take a salary cut. You have to talk the talk, and walk the walk. Only then will the rank and file realize what belt tightening is all about. Sacrifices have to be made at all levels, and the CEO has to set the example.

Everyone has to realize that there is a need to work longer hours, take less salary, do multiple jobs and be more flexible. In these times, you can't say, "This is not my job." An engineer may have to do quality control and a production manager may have to do maintenance jobs. All this has to be achieved while maintaining quality, because that is one factor that cannot change, in good times or bad. In fact, quality should improve in bad times to increase competitiveness.

The Bottom Line

Downsizing is normal, even essential, in business. It happens, and should happen, every three to five years. That it hasn't happened for ten years doesn't mean that it shouldn't or wouldn't have happened. It should be accepted as a routine cycle. That's the main reason everybody should have a cushion for the future. People must save for bad times, because they are going to come! Unfortunately, due to the extended period of growth, people have forgotten what saving is all about. We grew up with the idea of saving, even in the good times, because we knew that bad times would come. In fact, earlier there were often more bad times than good times. Now it is the other way around. People and companies have spent indiscriminately and the present situation teaches a good lesson. People have bought homes, for example, and are now having problems making mortgage payments because they never thought that a slowdown would hit them.

The situation is going to rapidly get worse, because now the reality is setting in. Increasing unemployment is drastically reducing spending. Corporate revenues of some high-tech companies are slowing to 50 percent of their peak levels, an unthinkably high number. This means the workforce will have to be reduced by 50 percent. The repercussions of this entire chain of events are huge.

In all of this, downsizing is painful, but crucial. It's like surgery — it hurts and it requires courage. But those who endure the surgery have a better chance of survival. Any measures that reduce expenses or increase cash flow are fair game. Decisions need to be made strictly on cash flow — not on ambition, emotion, or even regular business logic. It's all about how much cash you have and how much you need to survive. It's about keeping the doors open no matter how tough it gets out there.

■

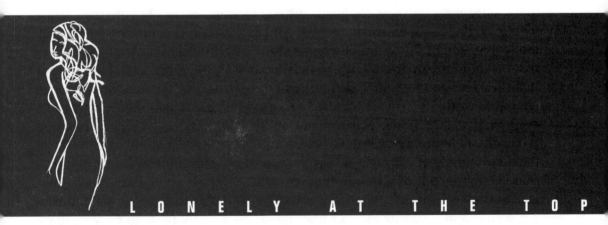

LONELY AT THE TOP

It is pretty lonely at the top. The higher you get in the management structure - social, political or business, the lonelier it gets. Let us talk about why that is, and what can be done about it - if there is anything that can be done.

P eople in organizations tend to believe that proximity is power. And I am not just referring to business — it is true of politics, family and any organization, for that matter. If you are the head of the organization, people want to be closer to you — physically. I remember in Indian Prime Minister Rajiv Gandhi's time, people shouted from the rooftops about how much time they spent with the PM. Perceived bonding: "Hey, I spent an hour with the PM." Time spent with the boss is generally perceived as a closeness index. The more time he spends with the boss, the more powerful he seems. What is it going to cost you as boss? You will have obsequious people who drag you through thirty minutes for work worth five minutes. It is called vicarious power — "I spent a lot of time with the boss, the boss is close to me."

People's Leader

And if that does not call for a time-out, you have to deal with people constantly trying to push their point of view when they talk to you. This is perhaps the truest in corporate structures. The marketing guy will always say marketing is fine, but the product guy messed up. The product guy will say the product's great, but marketing was no good. When someone comes to you, they come with an agenda — a personal agenda. And as a boss at the top, you have to listen, while being fully aware of what is really motivating him. And you have to make sure that you are taking enough interest in the guy's agenda that he is not offended. You hear him out, but you have to decide, depending on who is talking to you: "Do I divide this by two, or do I divide it by three?" If you take everybody at face value, you will not be able to make a decision. So, when proximity is being perceived as power and when people are always pushing their own points of view, the guy at the top has to play Sphinx. It is tough. But there is no way out of a system that requires you to be open, fair and egalitarian, when that is exactly what you cannot be. You play King Solomon and people will misunderstand you. So how much do you share, who do you share with and when?

Compounding your problem, is the "what you say" versus "what they hear" issue. What you say as a boss may get distorted through the employee's filter. He hears from his angle. If he is a marketing guy, he may assume you are telling him to push marketing all the way, when you are really not.

Then there is the whole issue of confidentiality. People will come to you and talk about other people. This kind of local politics seeps through every organization, even the family. If you are too open, and tell one person what the other said, you will break one's trust and the other's confidence. At the top, you have to listen to everybody. So, do not share too much, and make up your mind. But you will be walking a lonely road. You cannot really share everything with everybody. From your vantage point at the top, you see things very differently from the people below you. They see a microcosm of their own activities; you see a macrocosm of multiple activities. You have to integrate it all — and you are the only one who can.

Why Climb?

And while you are at it, you are essentially doing two things simultaneously — trying to manage peoples' personal aspirations and develop a consensus. Everyone in your organization has individual aspirations. And you are the sounding board for what they are doing and how they are feeling. At the same time, you are developing a consensus of all the different points of view. Also, you are the only one who can judge the value of performance versus promise. Everybody in the organization thinks they are more valuable then they really are. Everybody promises, but you judge the performance. You know that when one guy says he will get something done, he will get it done. And when another guy promises to deliver, chances are he will just finish half way. You are the one setting those perimeters. And if you start sharing that with everybody, you create problems in the organization. You have to make the judgment between types of people and their utility. Everybody thinks they are not getting their due recognition and credit. And credit and recognition, to them, means you agreeing with them a hundred percent of the time. You cannot do that and hope to run an organization. So whenever you make a decision, you are making enemies at the same time — no matter what decision it is. If somebody has been sidelined, he will think, "He did not listen to my advice, and he never does." You cannot listen to everybody's advice on everything. You feel bad because you do not want to hurt anybody, but in the decision making process, you are going to have to step on some toes.

That puts you on the spot. You want to keep everybody happy, because that is how you motivate them — unhappy people are difficult to motivate. So while you are spreading happiness and good cheer, you have to be fair to the organization. But if you are in the business of keeping everybody happy, you will not get anything done. It is a very complicated balance, and that is why it is lonely at the top — there is nobody else to maintain that balance. You are isolated and you are alone. Also, people are constantly bringing you their problems. Even good news ends with a problem — "this is working fine, but this needs fixing." Enormous amounts of people need you to solve their problems. They do not assume that you have problems too. After all, you are the guy at the top.

Once you recognize that loneliness at the top is a given, you learn to deal with it. You make the best out of it. One thing that has helped me a great deal is my group of friends outside of business with whom I share things about business. I have a group of friends with whom I share things about my family. All this happens at an intellectual level, since they are not involved in it. That has helped me a lot personally. You can sit down with some friends who have nothing to do with your business and talk shop with them. When it is a group of people with no vested interests, then it is easier for them to be more objective. You can bounce ideas off them.

At the end though, you have to accept it – it is lonely up there. So why climb to the top? Because it exists.

■

JUST CHILL

In an increasingly hectic work environment, it is extremely important to maintain focus on the things that really count.

Our work has a tendency to eclipse the rest of our identity. We introduce ourselves to others by saying, "I am a lawyer," or "I am a banker," and sometimes forget that we are actually so much more. Professional achievement is important, but it is dependent on a more fundamental sort of success. In today's fast paced work place, because of the emphasis on IT and the whole transformation that is taking place, people are constantly in a rush. They have to manage family life, work, health, interpersonal relationships and a host of other complications. Because of our fixation on items that are immediately pending, we lose sight of the things that really count, which provide us with the energy and purpose for our work. Throughout my career, I have constantly attempted to find a balance between the immediate and the permanent, between the ephemerally important and the things that count in the long run. Here are a few lessons that I have learnt.

Beauty in Chaos

With all the pressure at work, I constantly need to focus on three core areas: the self, family, and friends. Ultimately, I draw all the energy I need to work from these sources. It begins with the "self." I think I have been influenced more – consciously and subconsciously – by the Eastern concept of self than the Western. The Eastern concept, to me, is more holistic, and is comfortable with chaos. It accepts chaos as a part of life. Growing up in India, your eyes see an Indian mosaic of disparate things. You see placid water buffaloes and a swank Mercedes on the same dirt road, with little kids gawking at its gleaming exterior. A colorful drama is always played out in front of you. The culture is full of variety and of course, constant chaos. Yet you feel comfortable in the midst of this – people eat in the streets, they enjoy their environment. In the West, everything seems compartmentalized. People associate with people of their own age, their own type, and organize playgroups for their kids. In India, you cut diagonally across these lines. The elderly tell stories to children and if you miss the bus, you just hop onto your friend's scooter. You are a part of everybody's life, and not just in your own compartment. I believe these images have played an important role in my adult life. They teach us to live with chaos, to realize that life has its ups and downs and is not always very structured. Having learnt to appreciate these instances of chaos has given me a great sense of comfort in trying times.

Do Your Work, Through Thick and Thin

You have to have stable self-esteem, or else you cannot maintain your efficiency. In India, you often have to have an alligator thick skin. People poke and prod. If they draw blood, they poke even more. You have to have a firmly grounded sense of self; otherwise you will be in trouble. If your boss passes a not too positive comment on to you, you will not be able sleep at night. If things are not going well, you get uptight. You cannot let these things get to you, because in the larger scheme of things, they are insignificant. What is important today will seldom be important tomorrow, just as newspaper headlines from yesterday are forgotten the day after. People have a short memory span; so do not worry about what others will say. If it feels good, it must be good. Just do it.

Another thing I have absorbed from India is the concept of karma, by which I mean the philosophical principle more than the religious doctrine. You do things because they need to be done, without looking to see what they can do for you. It is another way of looking at the self. Your actions should not simply be coded into an equation, which you hope will yield a positive output. You should concentrate on doing your job well and not worry about the fruits of your labor. Cement this with a sense of discipline. If you are disciplined – when you write down things, follow up on things, keep yourself organized — then work becomes clearer. You can have a tighter assessment of your performance. This wider picture really keeps you balanced. Stay focused on the future, because the present is just a journey to get to where you want to eventually be.

The Human Community

After the self, there is the family. Wife, children, siblings, parents, grandparents, aunts and uncles – you derive energy from all these different people. You derive energy from the young and wisdom from the old. And after a hard day of work you know you can put your feet up in your favorite corner and you can just drop in at your uncle's house without calling ahead. There is a place to go and there are people to meet. Even if you are having a bad day, they will accept you. You can share in their joys and sorrows. This is the beauty of human community, and man is a social animal. Family is the reviving epicenter of your day's joys and frustrations. To me, the quality of time spent with the family is more important than the quantity of time. I do not often get to spend extended time with my family, but the quality of our time is always excellent. Wherever I am, I try to keep in touch with my family – even if it is for a few brief moments.

Good friends are a crucial aspect of my life. I think that if you do not have good friends, you should reexamine your life. This does not just mean like-minded friends, but friends of all types. I have friends who are diametrically opposite to me in many ways. I have a group of very religious friends, though I am not a religious man and a group of hard-wired intellectuals – at times I cannot even relate to their conversations. I have one friend who is heavily involved in the Rama Krishnan mission. I have friends that are sportsmen and doctors. And I have learned something from all of them. My psychiatrist friend taught me invaluable lessons about interpersonal relationships. It is very important to have friends who like you for who you are, people you can joke with and cry with. Sometimes, in taking care of our relationships and affairs, we forget to take care of ourselves. But it is very important not to forget to take care of your health – it is the beginning of happiness.

Self, family and friends. The three are crucial in maintaining balance in your life, and focus on things that really matter. Our immediate successes and failures sometimes absorb us completely. My father had told me that life was a journey, and you have to experience the entire journey. There is often a fine line that separates our perception of success from failure, and it is drawn quite arbitrarily. Rather than concern ourselves with the results that our actions will yield, we should concentrate on doing our jobs well and maintaining happiness. Real success is sure to follow.

■

CHANGE OF GUARD

In today's difficult times, it's common to see companies make changes at the top management level. It is important to understand such changes of guard, not only from the new leader's perspective on the process of creating a new enterprise, but also from the perspective of how people perceive the leader, their jobs and their future.

Corporate employees who understand their corporation's objectives generally accept that if the company under-performs, change is needed.

To understand the perspective of a new CEO, it is necessary to understand the particular executive – his or her background, style, experience and track record. There are three broad types of senior executives – analytical, corporate and entrepreneurial. It is crucial to understand to which category the new incumbent belongs.

Is he analytical – more of the management consultant type who relies on dynamic facts, figures and industry trends? Or is he a corporate type – who brings the staff together, creates teamwork, keeps position in place, and works toward organizational structure? Or is he the entrepreneurial type – dynamic, highly inspirational, but may have an unstructured approach, and often be rash with goals and systems.

It is also crucial to take into account this new leader's age. Is he young and thus needs to prove himself? Or is he more mature, with a proven track record, and may not need to prove anything to anybody? Further, you may ask, how did he really arrive at this job? Was he picked by a powerful board member? Chosen via executive search? Or did he come in as part of merger or acquisition? It's very important to understand this person, to understand his approach to change.

Finding Your Place

As a new CEO or senior executive, you have to carefully consider how to approach change. Take some time out to listen closely to people in the organization, no matter how much time it takes. That means talking to all functional groups - marketing, development, strategy, customers, quality, and so on. Everyone will have a different view of how the firm got into trouble and what is needed to get back on track. Where did we go wrong? Who is to be blamed? What could have been done earlier? By listening, you will develop your own view of what needs to be done.

If you don't listen closely and form your judgments too quickly, you could miss the important signals coming through the noise. Initially, there will be a lot of mistaken impressions generated by your new staff's emotions. People may say things they later regret and complain about irrelevant issues. You need to work through this and focus on the core issues. After you decide what's needed, you should discuss it with those who matter. You need to get stakeholders to buy into your strategy. If you don't, few people will cooperate with you. There's always a need for balance between changing too quickly or too slowly.

Once you have listened, analyzed, consulted and decided, you're ready to communicate with clarity to all the people associated with the company. This is the time to call a major meeting where you confidently announce what it is you are going to do. In the announcement, don't focus too much on the long-term. Instead, focus on the next 100 days. That will build confidence and minimize fear.

Leaders who follow a systematic, organized strategy will have an easier time implementing change. To lay off or fire people randomly is not a prudent answer. In this way, people will also feel that the guy at the top is willing to listen and understand their problems, and act for the larger good. It will be perceived as setting a rational course, rather than acting on whim or personal preferences.

The Employee's Perspective

If you are an employee at a company, get this: change is inevitable. Your new superiors may change products, policies or programs. The key is not to look at the past, but rather the future. Comparisons of past performance with tomorrow's plans makes people feel uneasy because they are comfortable with the way things used to work. But that old way got the company into trouble.

Change is part of a successful company's life. Help the new CEO make necessary changes by accepting them, embracing them, because they will create a new future that will be better. It's going to be painful. The CEO may make decisions that you will not agree with because you are used to doing it one way. But if he continues to do things the same way there will be no change and nothing will be accomplished.

So give him time and your support. He may not understand your business as fast as you expect him to. He's only been there for a short period of time, and you may have been there for many years. But that's his strength! To some extent, there is power in not being aware of all the nitty-gritty details.

Respect him for his lack of understanding. In tough times, employees can help the company by avoiding panic and not becoming a part of the rumor mill. Keep communications open. Confrontations, either between individuals or within a department, should be resolved quickly, before they spread and involve everybody, because conflict could render the new leadership ineffective.

This change of guard process is a "people process," more than one of performance, product or priority. Invariably, it starts within the company. Everyone knows what needs to be done, but somehow it doesn't get done. There's no real focus, no leadership, no desire to change. You've just somehow gotten into this mess and somebody has to make some changes.

Egos also play a major role when changes are implemented. Department heads may take a look at the new CEO and think, "How dare he say this to me?" CEOs need to massage everyone's ego to make sure they remain effective. Otherwise, some people who are hung up on their old position, rather than excited about their new responsibility, will become ineffective.

The new leader is certain to make changes in the organization. He's going to put some people on the side and some people on top and some people on the bottom. Some people won't be affected. If you stay optimistic and enthusiastic, and you perform well, even if the CEO makes a mistake and sidelines you, over a period of time he'll recognize that and correct it. If you react then and there, you'll make his job very difficult.

People are a company's biggest assets, especially in the knowledge business. Change of guard is a very complicated and delicate human process, and a great testing ground for leadership and integrity.

■

B E Y O N D   J U S T   B U S I N E S S

Growing a business, making it profitable, going public, expanding internationally - these are stages in the life of a company. But doing "good business" also means doing ethical business, which is governed by the philosophy and approach of the company's management.

"I think many people assume, wrongly, that a company exists solely to make money." —David Packard, co-founder of Hewlett Packard

The Equity Issue

In my mind, the fundamental issue in business ethics is equity for people at large. For multinational companies, responsibility is not simply due to the people of the country in which they are doing business, but also lies in other parts of the world in which they do business: Africa, Asia and Latin America. In this sense, equity does not mean an equitable distribution of wealth – a company cannot provide this to a population. Rather, a company can improve the standard of living for a large number of people that it touches through its products and services — whether those are telephone services, financial services, gasoline or soap. To fulfill their responsibility to the population, a company must be accountable to all consumers who use their products and services.

From the equity issue stems the idea of values. Personal values are no different from business values – they apply to conduct, integrity, environment and ecology, economics and every other issue that affects businesses. Acting upon good values is not an option, but should play a critical role in all corporate decisions and subsequent actions. The equity issue has always been a volatile topic; emerging from the rhetoric and debate is a fledgling recognition that social development is crucial to sustainable development.

Up until this epiphany, sustainable development was viewed in terms of environmental protection and resource conservation. Global warming, loss of biodiversity and lack of resource conservation were the main concerns. Developing nations agree that citizens of developed nations can afford to be concerned with the fact that rain forests and sea lions are going the way of dinosaurs. These concerns, however, are luxuries allowed to countries that are not primarily focused on simply surviving, economically, ecologically and socially.

Why is the equity issue in the spotlight? In 1960, the richest fifth of world population netted 70.2 percent of world income; the poorest fifth netted 2.3 percent. In 1995, the richest fifth secured 86.0 percent of world income; the poorest fifth managed 1.1 percent. Obviously, the equity gap is increasingly becoming a steep and treacherous ravine.

A 1997 document, entitled The Program For The Further Implementation Of Agenda 21, issued by the United Nations following the Rio +5 conference held in New York in 1997, states: "Economic development, social development and environmental protection are interdependent and mutually reinforcing components of sustainable development. Sustained economic growth is essential to the economic and social development of all countries, in particular developing countries."

People-centered Economics

Can worldwide economic growth deliver on the promise of globally sustainable development? It can, if it is on a track of people-centered economics, not just corporate-centered economics. Growth is not simply about products and services, it is also about what people get out of them and to what extent their well-being is considered. There is the need to search for the soul of business. This dictates the value of businesses, which in turn dictates social responsibility.

Well, these ideas make for great slogans. Corporate executives often articulate these issues, but in reality, execution is difficult and has been lacking. Executive viewpoints may come up against shareholder values, which typically question less-than-profitable actions. For example, why should money that constitutes a mere one-percent of the profit of a company be spent on education? This is when senior management, especially the chief executive, needs to step in to fearlessly support the fact that spending one percent of the profit on educating children makes great business sense — because in the future, educated children become consumers with greater demands. A chief executive's support of these values will foster a natural percolation throughout the organization. So implementation of a higher value system will stand a stronger chance overall.

Ethical Audits

Part of the solution is that business ethics need to be institutionalized. Like financial audits, there is a need for internal and external "ethical audits." Internal ethical audits would raise awareness among employees. External audits create outside pressures for companies to execute these programs effectively. In today's cutthroat, financially driven world, people who talk about business ethics are considered "activists" or "crusaders" — simply not fair judgment given the fundamental nature of these issues, as they are the responsibility of both big and small players.

Broad-based Efforts

The best way to improve standards of living is not really through the UN and other non-profit organization programs, but through corporate efforts. Large, highly profitable companies may be involved in these efforts, with their participation based mostly on their financial muscle. Other companies have creative ways of encouraging social awareness. Companies that do business in a specific region will have better insight into the local area, people and problems of that geographic area. There is no reason why the world's largest and smallest companies cannot decide to make this world literate and healthy. This is the big picture — a long-term view of the world. And it is a win-win situation.

In Francis Kinsman's recent book, *Millennium*, he sees society as divided into three main categories: sustenance driven, outer directed and inner directed. The sustenance driven citizens struggle to make ends meet. Their main concern is to have a better standard of living. The outer directed group has all its basic needs met. The people in this group measure their status in society in terms of their economic affluence. This group will probably be indifferent to the concept of sustainable development. Inner directed people are more value driven than the others; their lifestyles and consumption patterns reflect this. Members of this group are likely to be more receptive toward the concept of sustainable development.

Applying these terms to companies, a sustenance driven company's biggest battle would be to break even. An outer directed company, one motivated purely by balance sheets, would probably limit its responsibility to economic development. An inner directed company that is more values driven would adopt an inclusive approach toward shareholders and support sustainable development. As we should aim to be Inner directed citizens, companies should also seek to achieve inner direction — this is social capitalism at its best.

In the coming few years, companies need to reinvent themselves to become more inner directed. Multinational companies should use their business clout and resources to support frameworks for sustainable development set up by governments. Values need to change for the better in society and also among the leaders in the upper echelons of management. The bottom line is that long-term strategies focusing on socio-ecological problems have to be developed concurrently with short-term commercial goals.

There is nothing more difficult to plan, more doubtful of success, nor more dangerous to manage than the creation of a new system. For the initiator has the enmity of all who would profit by the preservation of the old institutions, and merely lukewarm defenders in those who should gain by the new ones. — Machiavelli

■